TOM'S BOOK

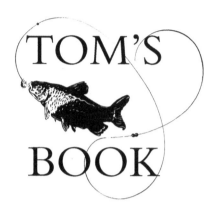

For Tom.

TOM'S BOOK

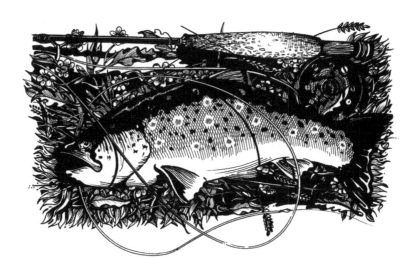

A COLLECTION OF
FISHING STORIES

by

ROBERT OLSEN

DESIGNED AND ILLUSTRATED
BY THE AUTHOR

FOREWORD *by* JOHN BAILEY

First published in Great Britain, 2011.
Paperback first published in Great Britain, 2013.

Text and Illustrations © Robert Olsen, 2011.

ISBN 978-0-9574283-3-1

Designed and illustrated by Robert Olsen.

Typeset in 11/15pt Bembo.

CONTENTS

CONTENTS

Do not for a moment think I am name dropping here because I am truly not. I've just been lucky to fish with acknowledged greats. I've seen John Wilson, Bob James, Chris Yates, Matt Hayes, Hugh Falkus, Arthur Oglesby, Dermott Wilson, Fred Taylor, Ivan Marks, Peter Stone and almost anybody you care to name from the later twentieth century in action. And what always worried me was the nagging thought that there are great anglers out there who never had the media exposure to thrust them into the spotlight, whatever that is in angling. Then, in 1990 or thereabouts, I met Rob Olsen and I knew I'd been right all along.

Rob fished like an angel – a hairy one, true. I can talk on one level about watercraft, float control, feeding patterns and all the usual stuff. I'd rather say that Rob was instantly recognisable as a real, true, line through the blood fisherman. It's about instinct. It's about poise. It's about a marriage with the water. Wherever the water is. Whatever the species. Whatever the method employed. It's a depth of feeling that Rob displayed that goes beyond all usual description.

I could tell endless stories about Rob's triumphs in Mongolia, in India, in Spain and all over the UK but he probably wouldn't want that. Anyway, he tells his stories better in his own words. Let's just say that if fish could speak, in their language Rob would be fluent.

Because he's totally in tune with water and what lives there, he writes beautifully. His illustrations are truly remarkable and show the same liquid affinity. And if all this isn't enough, you'd better know that he's generous with his praise and support. He's unassuming. He's full of fun. He's the greatest of friends.

What more could old Isaak have ever asked for? And no, I never fished with Walton!

THANK YOU

A fishing rod has taken me to some wonderful places and I have met many people along the way who have made all those early mornings and miles travelled worthwhile. Without them, the following collection of stories would not have been possible. Some of those people appear in these pages, many more made them happen. In particular I would like to thank the following:

Phil Humm for his infectious enthusiasm, friendship and ability to turn float fishing into art. John Bailey for his pioneering and for sharing his skills on rivers, ponds and puddles in this country and abroad. Ian Miller for allowing me access to a particularly interesting stretch of the river Wye and for his mastery of both the camp fire and Kelly kettle. Ade Bristow for the fly-fishing trips. John Gilman for the ones after just about anything that swims. Leo Grosze Nipper, Mick Bay, Ian Whitelaw, Alan Felstead, Dan Goff and Simon MacMillan for the overseas trips. John Ferebee and Nigel Pattison for the local ones. Mike Taylor at the Red Lion Hotel, Bredwardine, for the hospitality, the late Bernard Venables for his encouragement and special thanks to Rod Green for getting me back into fishing at a time when I thought there were more important things in life.

At home a big thank you to Helen for everything and especially for allowing me the freedom to fish. Oh, and of course, to my son, Tom, just for being Tom.

Thank you all for your belief.

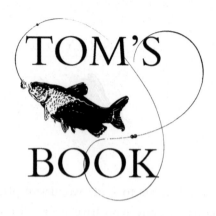

TOM'S BOOK

An obliging fish, a hook, a piece of thread and a bucket full of excitement bring fish and angler together creating a memory that is so iridescent, so addictive, that you want to repeat it over and over and over. Yet, even with all its glory, there is a dilemma attached to fishing. You crave to extend the moment, to hold the treasure from the depths, to absorb the sense of wonder and yet you don't want to harm the creation at the centre of your rapture. This is something that seems odd to some people, stupid to a few more and downright cruel to others and yet it is totally understandable to those of us who have experienced it.

A sense snaps into play. The same deep instinct that tells a child how to cup a butterfly in tiny hands before peeping, just once more, at a flake of Nature's genius before letting it go - it's called respect. It needs no schooling, religious instruction or television to programme feelings that ingrained. Every child does it. Every child smiles when they do it and every spectator approves of what they see. It's automatic and it's a reminder of how things should be.

In the brief moments I get beside the water, I try hard to catch those fish, always admire them and, like those children, I can't help smiling when I return them to their rightful environment. Smiling, you see, is what fishing is all about, the very core. It is immensely important. It is because the whole act of fishing is so calming, so pleasing, that it has to be communicated. Nature's narcotic has gripped me hard. No matter how many years pass, whenever I hold a fishing rod, I feel ten years old. That's the magic of it. It isn't complicated, hard or painful. It's fun.

An individual's fishing life is not an orderly list of fish caught or lost. It is a haphazard collection of events that bounce from rivers, ponds and streams and it is only once the ripples have subsided that any sense can be made of them. Good or bad days are hard to predict because there are so many elements that need to come together, both physical and emotional, to make the day a memorable one. When a fish crashes into your life it leaves a mark on your memory that is etched for eternity.

The following collection of stories are in no chronological order. They are plucked, randomly, like the fish themselves, from the wealth of enjoyment and fascination that surrounds my own fishing and I would like to dedicate them to all those people who have asked, 'Tell me, exactly why do you go fishing?' For all those I have bored when I've turned the subject around to what I've wanted to talk about, and, most importantly, for my growing son, just in case he doesn't find out what it's all about for himself.

For that last reason, the title of this book labelled itself as exactly what it's meant to be, a book for my son - TOM'S BOOK.

ONE FOR THE WALL

BARBEL - THE RIVER WYE

Occasionally everything fits into the plan even
when there wasn't really a plan in the first place.

I sat alone in the car with Neil Young. The drizzle on the windscreen was the light annoying type that is not enough to leave the wipers on, yet too much to switch them off. A small annoyance on an otherwise promising morning that started with a mug of tea in the kitchen and ended with a fish.

Having been travelling for fifteen minutes, I knew there was another fifty to go. It was dark outside but I could tell that the weather was easing. I had the whole day in front of me so I was in that state that Zen Buddhists call 'contentment'.

The tranquil image of the solitary fisherman should have had me listening to some classical piece (Mozart or Schubert perhaps) as I trundled along at a sensible speed taking life easy, absorbing every drip of an unfolding day. I thought about this image for a couple of minutes and then put good English leather hard down onto efficient Japanese engineering and turned up Neil Young - very loud.

It seemed right. I had been worrying about the clattering coming from the back of the car for too long. It was either a wheel working loose or two delicate fishing rods bouncing up and down damaging hook points, carbon fibre and bamboo in the process - the latter would have been worse but only just. Neil Young and Crazy Horse blotted out the worry, allowing me to think about more important things.

Country roads at this time in the morning are like the ones in a sixties B movie - quiet, empty, bumpy and a little dangerous. Lack of traffic should make them safer but you can be drawn into a false sense of security when you are one of the few people awake.

The odd fox, a wet patch of leaves, the village tom-cat and the police car that always appears in the rear view mirror when you're doing really well on the time front, all make you realise that you're far from immortal. You should take it easy, but you don't.

There should have been no hurry. For once I had the timing right. I had been thinking about the day, the prospects and the river all week - this time I would arrive before first light (just as they say you should in the books). This time I had a good feeling about the whole thing. Exactly why was hard to pin down, but I did. In between avoiding rabbits and the milkman just outside Holme Lacy, I had worked out exactly where I would fish. It was a judgement that wasn't based on barometric readings, light values or the previous evening's weather report (as it probably should have been). It was based on the fact that, 'Yep, that will be a fine place to fish.'

As I approached the river I drove over the old red brick bridge without stopping. There had always been this kind of ritual whenever I crossed that bridge. I had always pulled the car over, got out, surveyed the river, gazed meaningfully over the parapet, and then decided where on the river to fish first, whether it was dark or not. This time my mind was made up. I knew exactly where I was going. I was closing in on Eldorado a hell of a lot quicker than Cortez ever did.

Neil Young turned into Van Morrison, shortly after I turned onto the grass verge. As I did so I flicked off the CD player and listened hard to the silence. The only interruption was the ticking of the cooling engine. The lyrics of the last song had been crooning something along the lines of, 'Paradise must be something like this' and I thought, 'damn right Mr. Morrison'. At that moment I noticed it had stopped raining.

I would have got out of the car even if I didn't have to open the gate. I really wanted to be fishing, but it's necessary to hurry slowly when you are doing something this important. Besides, I like the gate. It pulls eagerness into perspective. It allows you to lean on it, to look around and to fumble with pieces of bailer twine. These things are important and without them we may as well just fish a stocked swimming pool.

People who barge through such obstacles are missing out on something worthwhile. This is a good gate too. I once thought about mending the sign but it hangs at an angle adding a degree of authority. I like that, there is no need to mess with niceties like 'would you mind awfully if you could close the gate after you'. It says, 'SHUT THE GATE,' so you shut the gate and you do it as quietly as cold metal and wood will allow and make sure that no livestock comes stampeding out of the darkness. Once you have done this you can rest assured in the fact that it is just as hard for anybody else to get in. I like that too. It's a fine feeling. Fishing and gates fit nicely together with a reassuring clunk.

I came across three types of creature before getting to the river. Sheep in the first field, cattle in the second and hoards of rabbits in both. It was too dark to see any buzzards circling around, but they would arrive once the thermals had warmed up.

On approaching the river I wanted to switch off the headlights for fear of spooking any fish (actually, I was more worried about spooking the ducks that would then spook the fish - the end result is the same). At the same time I didn't want to drive in and greet them in the river because I couldn't really see where I was going. I stopped the car to think it out.

Where I was heading for was a quarter of a river mile away. Having stopped the car, I got out, stretched a little, searched through the dark and wondered if I had brought along any bait. When I opened up the car boot I realised that, in the event of getting stranded anywhere in the country, I could probably survive for at least a week before contemplating trying to kill one of those rabbits. A diet of corn, luncheon meat, stale bread, hemp, pedigree chum mixers, worms and boiled pigeon feed may not sound that appetising but there is usually a can or two of warm beer rattling around in there too.

I changed my boots, dug out the hat and selected a rod. It was like choosing which sabre to use in a dual. I hesitated for a moment before selecting the old cane one. The line was threaded through the guides and the hook whipped on in the dark. Even though it is an old rod I had only just finished renovating it from the sorry state I found it in, tucked away amongst some more saleable split cane fly rods in a junk shop. It didn't look that pretty but it only cost me £12 so I reckoned that, even taking into account several weeks work to get it back into fishable use, I had got myself a bargain. In this way it was old, but new, heavier than the other one, but far more aesthetic – it was a nice morning – the choice was right. I started walking.

A blackbird sparked off the dawn chorus. The sky turned magenta. My eyes focused with the growing light and stayed there as I dropped down a high bluff (where only fishermen and thirsty cattle go) then, at last, I was able to pick out the river. The trees on the opposite bank and the wall of dusty soil behind me tunnelled the vision, highlighting what I had come all this way to experience. Automation clicked in.

Sneaking across a beach of gravel, I released the hook from the retaining eye on the renovated rod, nipped two swan shot onto a link of line, tested a very dubious slipping clutch on the reel and loaded the hook with three grains of sweet corn. The first grain was slid over the hook eye and then back down to cover the knot and eye of the hook. A minor detail that may or, may not, make a difference. It's one of those things I always do.

I left my small fishing bag half way across the gravel, the landing net three quarters of the way across and crouched down, inching forward until some warm water trickled over the top of my left boot. I retreated a few inches and made the first cast of the day.

When using sweet corn as a bait, it is generally accepted that you have to get the fish interested in it in the first place by giving them a couple of handfuls to try first. I prefer to try a few casts before jumping into this approach. If you are pretty sure of where the fish will be on that day, there is every likelihood that one will be caught first cast. It has happened this way for me on enough occasions to give me the confidence to make the cast. This morning it didn't. But that exploratory cast had enabled me to get a clearer picture of the river bed and how the currents were working across it on that particular day. Now I could introduce some free offerings with a fair chance of getting it right. Then I moved up the river twenty yards and tried under some bushes, with a lobworm. I then tried another place. Then another. In between failing to catch fish, I returned to my original choice and introduced a few more grains of corn. Six or seven at a time seemed enough.

It was turning into a fine day. The sun was creeping above the tree line and the place I had baited looked even more promising as it became one of the few patches of water that retained any shade.

Time for another cast.

That cast was like something out of a movie. Bugs coming off the surface, sun breaking through the foliage, dappled water sliding across the scene, panoramic vision, slow motion poetry. The lead beads split the water with a little 'clump'. The line bowed, I mended it back upstream, the bait bounced and then settled. I took up the slack, felt a pluck that felt different to any other the river had fooled me with that morning and I struck into a fish. At that moment I thought I saw a kingfisher flash past and heard the peel of distant church bells – I could have been mistaken.

The act was played out in full theatre even though there was no audience to applaud. That fish fought hard and then harder again. Then she was in the net. That is all I can say about my moment of glory, the rest is very private and only comes out at night when I'm trying to turn nightmares in to dreams.

She was a lovely creature, bright, muscular and of a size that would almost impress the weekly angling papers. She deserved a photograph and I took plenty, for all that time I had been thinking in the car on the way to the river I kept promising myself that if I ever caught a barbel over ten pounds in weight that I would do a painting of her - life size.

When I eventually retired to the local bar for lunch I sat, very happily, by the window and sketched out her portrait on the scrap of paper I had taken from my back pocket. I drew her outline, decided to include the old rod and reel that had overpowered her and scribbled a caption beneath that read 'Barbel, 10lb. 4oz. Caught from the river Wye with an 11ft. Wallis Wizard rod, Ambidex reel and three grains of sweet corn.'

It was the first fish I had caught on the renovated rod. Although this all happened over fourteen years ago I haven't finished the painting. The rod hangs above the desk in my studio. I still use it when I get that feeling of certainty that crops up every now and again. I didn't fish that afternoon.

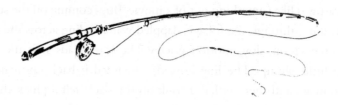

ADDER CORNER

CARP - THE FOREST OF DEAN

*Statistics tell me that fishing is way up there with
the world's most dangerous sports.
I can understand that.*

It was an extremely small fish. A pike. Made from enamel and painted
unrealistically. Helen had bought it for me from one of those craft stalls
in Covent Garden and it had been attached to the lapel of my old
fishing coat ever since. The tail had become severely bent. The paint had
chipped. The pin was working loose and it was looking old. I liked it. It
had this strange attraction.

You may recognise this situation. You're leaning on the bar in the
local pub, minding your own business, like a good boy. A stranger slides
up, spots the badge, and pronounces, 'You go fishing then?' The stranger
stands a good chance of getting into a conversation unless you went for
a beer in the first instance to get away from people like this. As it turns
out you get to talking about a common interest. Once you're passed the,
'What type of fishing?' 'How big?' And, 'What type of rod do you use?'
The conversation cuts to the core as it turns to different types of water.
Some you have fished, the interesting ones are those that you haven't -
yet.

This is a good way to find out about new waters but it is also
impossible to plan. Like all the best things, they just happen. If you read
about a new location to fish, you can be sure that the entire circulation of
the publication have done the same thing, so, there's more than a chance
that when you get around to visiting them they are already over fished.

When your idea of an overcrowded water is when there is somebody else there, you're on to a loser. No, it's the secret places you're more interested in, the places that creep into your twilight thoughts, the places that chance meetings like this can unearth.

Some of these leads seem impossible. Some too good to be true. And others come from people who have never even held a fishing rod but you still make an attempt to follow them up because you never really know. Disappointment becomes regular yet the more you probe the more chance you have of finding that dream water and, most of the time, it is just a dream.

The conversation at the bar became interesting as the man started to loosen up as his glass emptied. 'There's a couple of small pools,' he said. 'Hidden in the middle of the Forest of Dean. Overgrown. Inaccessible. Not many people know about them. Some nice carp in there though. You never see anyone else there. The banks are uneven and you can't even find a decent spot to put your chair. Quite a walk too.'

This man liked talking, didn't like the place and was only talking about it because he had been somewhere that I hadn't. But (and this is the important thing to remember) what one person considers bad may well be your idea of heaven. The badge had worked again.

It cost me one of those large scale Ordinance Survey maps that you can only buy in the posh book shops but I found the place in the end. Two tiny blobs of blue surrounded by a great deal of green that reminded me how excited you can get over little things.

On a chilly morning in January I went to have a look at those pools. I had to leave my car by the padlocked entrance, climb over a cold metal gate and walk half a mile through a dark pine forest following a deeply rutted track that was designed to destroy the average family car and to break ankles when you've got out to push. It was spooky in there too, particularly when I came across a rusty old sign nailed upon a dead tree that I couldn't quite read but knew it once said something along the lines of, 'Trespassers will be shot.'

I smelt the water before I saw it. As soon as I saw it I knew that I would have to fish it.

There were the two pools, surrounded by statuesque evergreens. The top one was roughly triangular with a dam at one end and extensive shallows at the other. The whole place was sheltered by those trees. The still surface of the water reflected the surroundings like a mirror. The second pool was similar if not a little more overgrown. So pristine. So quiet. Just perfect. It smelt old. I saw no fish but they were there. Sometimes you can just tell.

After a bit of poking about I came across a small wooden hut covered in ivy and an old fibreglass rowing boat with a large hole in the bottom discarded around the back. Hammered in the ground was a notice declaring – 'STRICTLY PRIVATE FISHING'. Contradicting this statement was a footnote that included a telephone number that suggested, 'We don't really want you here but if you've got enough money we just might'. I had to remember that number until I got back to the car where I could write it down and bundle it in the glove compartment with all the others. It was a good morning's trespassing.

I made that telephone call, met a man by the gate early the following weekend and parted with a considerable sum of money. I had to walk through the woods to get over the shock.

I was granted permission to fish for the remainder of the season from the following week (which meant they wanted to make sure the cheque didn't bounce) but once I was sure the owner had left I couldn't resist a cast or two and seeing as how he'd spotted the rod in the back of the car I'm sure he knew I wasn't just going to walk away. For the record I didn't catch a thing.

On the way back I checked out the village pub on the reasoning that I'd be coming up here quite often. The bolts on the pub door had only just been cranked back. Low winter light cut through the previous evening's nicotine and hung as heavy as the mist that had hovered over the pools five hours previously. Having scraped the majority of mud off my boots, I walked in and politely ordered a Guinness.

'We only sell English beer in here - boy.' Came the sharp reply from behind the bar.

'Right, I'll have a pint of English beer then.'
It took me a while to settle down after that and I just sat in the empty bar room by the unlit fire in some weird hope that it may give me some comfort.

It wasn't long before a beat-up pickup truck rolled up outside with three lurchers tied to the tailgate. Two men (late twenties, early thirties, wearing checked work shirts, long hair and steel toe-capped work boots) stomped in and looked at me for what I considered longer than necessary. They were pulled a couple of pints of 'English beer,' without having to ask for them. They then dragged up two heavy wooden chairs across the flagstone floor with a screech, deposited them at my table with a thump and asked, 'How you doing, Butt?'

The smaller one rested a rusty double barrel shotgun against the fireplace. Putting a tangible distance between the firearm and myself made me feel a little easier, but not much. The bright orange bailer twine tied around the stock and the barrel made a handy sling. It also made it fairly obvious that they hadn't retired early from the organised Sunday morning clay pigeon shoot for a glass of dry sherry and a slice of quiche.

They looked me up and down - slowly.

Spotting the little enamel badge one of them said,

'You fish then.'
It was a statement not a question but I was obliged to reply. The consequences of ignoring them could have been fatal.

'Yeah, I had an hour or two at those pools down the track.'

'Got permission to fish them?'

'Not exactly.'

'That's alright then.'

Having recognised I wasn't going to report them for poaching on the grounds that that was what I had been doing, we got on fine, but I still say that there are some strange people hidden in the Forest of Dean. The really worrying aspect is that they know it.

I fished down at those pools on a regular basis for the next few years. Caught quite a few fish too. It was nice. Leisurely. Almost spiritual. It was a good place to lose yourself and I got lost enough times in a year to make it worth paying the money. I got all romantic about the place too, started fishing with old split cane rods and centrepin reels, creeping about, stalking carp in the margins with bits of peacock quill for a float and fishing pieces of bread for the rudd when the carp weren't being cooperative.

My fishing consisted of a few hours snatched in the early mornings or after work. I stayed all day a few times, even all night on a couple of occasions, but the short visits suited me better. The intensity of the place could tire me out.

Now, I know that in this country there are very few things that can do you any serious harm outside of the city but the Forest of Dean is a weird place. One morning, when I had the pools to myself, I was disturbed by two free roaming Gloucester Blackspot pigs and I can tell you this, it is quite a shock when you come face to face with these critters through the early morning mist. They're a lot bigger than you'd think, they look at you for worryingly long periods of time and aren't that impressed when you poke them with an eleven foot, handmade, wooden fishing rod. They also leave you with the feeling that they'll be back.

But those pools were so pretty I kept going back whenever I got the time. The abundance of squirrels, birds, rabbits, badgers and even the odd deer were a picture book delight. It was the frogs that were the problem. Alright, I admit they're nice little creatures, totally harmless, kids love to catch them, but they also have you fooled into thinking that you've been stalking a margin feeding carp for the previous hour and that's a waste of good fishing time. Even so, the really serious problem with the frogs was that they attracted predators in numbers, and I mean big numbers.

A combination of the perfect location (quiet pine forest with a sun trap of two spring fed pools in the middle of it) and an abundance of food (all those frogs) attracted a large percentage of the surrounding area's snake population. There were some grass snakes in amongst them but the vast majority were adders. If there's one thing an adder likes it's frogs. I don't like snakes too much, and a fully grown adder is something that can hurt you – so I am reliably informed by my doctor.

Let me put my cards on the table and admit something here – they worried me. Hell, I was out there on my own most of the time. If I had been bitten I couldn't exactly flag down a passing ambulance and I didn't carry a mobile phone because fishing is all about losing yourself, not about being found. I'd been creeping about in the summer wearing a pair of shorts and making sure I was being as quiet as possible (so as not to scare the fish). As a result I came across a lot of snakes – generally I didn't hang about for too long to check whether they were one of the minority (the grass snakes) or the majority (the other kind).

I started humming and whispering things to myself in an attempt to make my presence known. This evasive action gave me a little more confidence until I watched a TV documentary about these things that not only showed me dramatic footage of adders striking their prey (very close up, wide-angle lens type shots) but also informed me of the fact I really needed to know at that time in my life – adders can not hear! Apparently, they detect everything through smell, vibration and sight. Great!

Vibration and being visible are the very things you want to avoid whilst stalking margin feeding fish. As the husky voiced narrator on the enlightening programme had pointed out - adders are very shy creatures and you will be lucky to actually see one. In fact, if one were to bite you (a situation which can bring on shock and a huge burst of adrenaline as the venom injects itself into your thinning bloodstream often resulting in heart failure) it was probably trodden on whilst it was asleep or you just happened to have been unlucky. Very reassuring! As for adders being rare? Well, on a summer's morning I could have shown you at least two within the first five paces of walking around those pools.

Now that I'm no longer fishing there, talking about those adders can make me feel pretty brave in a country-boy type of way. It enables me to say things like, 'So the place was crawling with venomous snakes - if you want to catch fish you have to put up with these sort of things.' I know this is bullshit but it can be quite impressive bullshit when you have got an audience who have never been out of bed before dawn. In a way, I did get used to those snakes but having came as close as you could without getting bitten, the thought of the possibility lives with me like some post-it note from above saying, 'Don't push your luck.'

It was a steaming hot, humid, dazzlingly bright day without a breath of wind. Not the best weather for carp fishing - but one that suited the resident snake population just fine.

I had set a little trap for a particular fish that visited the tiny lily covered bay at the far end of the pool where a stream trickled in and dragon flies hovered like combat helicopters. To be frank, I didn't expect the fish to fall for such an obvious tactic but she did. I suppose the smell of the floating bait was just too much for her because she materialised from the deeper water and drifted very slowly towards it. At first I followed her path by the nudging of the lily pads. Then I saw her quite clearly. She was a big, golden armoured, carp. She looked suspicious, but interested. She hung in liquid animation for an eternity before her fins began to flutter as she angled her body skyward. Crouched behind the reeds I was so close that I could see her eye swivel. She was hypnotized. She could resist it no longer.

At times like this your heart races and you forget the cramp in your legs. You reach, very slowly, for the rod you left next to yourself on the grass whilst trying to keep an eye on what's going on out there in the water. She was about to absorb the trap so I made my reach as I had done so many times before but something made me glance at the rod as I did so. My hand was about four inches away from the rod butt and curled up in a little dip underneath the old centrepin reel was a bloody great adder. I suppose I should have calmly retracted my hand (as the level headed chap on the TV documentary would have done). Instead I jumped one way, the snake arrowed the other and the carp bolted beneath the calm. It was a loud display of absolute panic by all involved. Both the carp and the snake made a full recovery. I'm not sure I have and this all happened quite a few years ago. Mankind just isn't meant to travel that fast.

Those snakes were always a concern during the summer but I still had some good times down at those pools. Although they were relatively close to home, they were far enough away to get the adrenaline pumping on a Friday night. Small enough to be embracing, large enough to be a challenge. Most of all the place was calming and, for the most part, left alone. The banks were overgrown and always appeared fresh, just how carp pools are meant to be.

Then the owners of the place got a little ambitious and they set about creating a better fishery. I reasoned that it was fine just as it was, but then I wasn't consulted. Out came the undergrowth and down went the little gravel paths. In the middle of a drought it was decided to drain the top pool and remove the snags that the fish liked but the other anglers didn't. The place had a complete overhaul and generally it's best not to fiddle about with Nature because she's pretty much in tune as she is. I can't say that I liked what I saw. Seeing that some of my money had helped to ruin what I had considered to be a special place, I left on what you could call 'favourable terms'. My reasoning for this was that, after a few years, when the paths have become overgrown again and a few more trees have fallen back into the place, it might be worth fishing again. I'm all for idyllic looking places to fish but I draw the line when they start getting the lawn mower out.

It hurt seeing the pools raped of their innocence and I don't like seeing things in pain. My affection for the place evaporated. I haven't been back (apart from to check whether the snakes are still there) so I've lost something that I held quite dear. Oddly enough, I lost the little pike badge around about the same time.

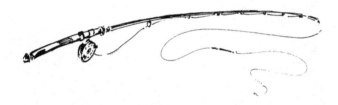

IT JUST ISN'T CRICKET

GRAYLING & TROUT - WALES

Beer and fishing go so well together that it surprises
me that more people don't fall in.

As I drive towards Builth Wells, the road narrows and begins to follow the Wye as it slices through the surrounding hills. Glimpses of the river bounce through the trees like a psychedelic light show. It gets a little dangerous as I try to judge the level and condition of the water whilst driving at 60 miles per hour. Anticipation and excitement have a habit of speeding you up, even though the reason I came up here in the first place was to slow down. Entering Erwood, I stamp on the brakes, lurch to the right and cut through a narrow opening flanked by dry stone walls. The back end of the car slides a little as I hit the mud track. I nearly always miss that entrance.

I open the door and step onto a light frost. I have the river to myself so I have a stretch and take time to reacquaint myself with the view.

It's spectacular. That's why someone built a wooden fishing hut up here. Actually, 'hut' is too small a description, whereas 'lodge' is too grand. It sort of sits in the middle - a very desirable 3 to 4 bedroom wooden structure with running water and electricity. On the roof there is a natty cast iron weather-vane depicting a fisherman that confirms that the morning is still. On the inside, huddled around the sleeping quarters, there is a kitchen, bathroom and a lounge area with French doors that open onto decking and a view to die for. I have never been inside (it's always locked) but I have strained through every window and keyhole just to get a better look at what I can't get access to. This place happens to be the deciding factor as to whether or not I buy a National Lottery ticket on Saturdays.

As I sat on the decking, the sun crept over the hill and illuminated the panorama in front of me as if the museum curator had turned up the dimmer switch so I could get a better look at the Mona Lisa. I wasn't disappointed either.

There's a long lazy bend in the river here, where the water looks smooth. It then narrows and gathers momentum as it slides over gravel before deepening and cascading through pools until it gushes past boulders the size of a three man dome tent, throwing up spray like a galleon crashing through a force nine as it goes. It's a true freestone river up here and when the levels are high, you can hear the boulders grinding along the bottom. It is an experience that tends to slow your wading down. But now, as I look, she is a touch over summer level, running clear, with a tinge of green. Like an emerald.

I sat there for a while taking it all in, adjusting to the perspective and wondering what it must have been like in the glory days, when huge salmon ran and sturdy gentleman fished from the boards with heavy greenheart rods and a stout resolve. By the time I snapped out off my dreaming, the sun had melted the frost and there was no longer a need for the fleece. Remembering why I had just driven 75 miles, I went fishing.

It was wonderfully quiet down by the river with only the music of the water for company. I started with a team of nymphs in an attempt to find some fish. After a few hours I had only managed a couple of suicidal little brown trout, both of which came jiggling up to the surface attached to the shrimp pattern on the point, so the fishing was pretty slow really. Later in the morning a few dimples from rising grayling started to appear at the tail of a pool making it look as if it was just beginning to rain. As quickly as they started they stopped. Five minutes later a line of bubbles rolled across the current like marbles on a glass table and then an otter surfaced. It was a beautiful sight but that pretty much explained why the grayling had gone. Just to prove me wrong, the otter dragged one onto a rock on the opposite bank illustrating that he was a far better fisherman than me.

The morning trundled on by with the usual relaxation but no more fish, so I broke for lunch and walked back to the car where I returned the rod to the tube and pulled out the lighter one that I use for dry-fly work, on the reasoning that the grayling tend to switch onto surface (or just sub-surface) feeding as the afternoons progress. I grabbed some sandwiches and a packet of crisps, and sat on the decking of the fishing hut as if I owned it. Unwrapping the sandwiches I found that the sun had warmed the car and they had gone a little soggy as a result. They reminded me of family picnics 45 years earlier. Between swallows, I set up a sweet American-made, five piece, five weight rod and attached the reel, threaded the line, added the leader and then a small Grey Wulff as a searching fly. I then went to retrieve two small cans of beer from the river that I had wedged between some rocks in the morning so that (unlike the sandwiches) they would be nice and cool.

Initially I thought I was going crazy, I must have got the wrong rock, but no, the beer had gone. I said something short and very descriptive. Looking around for those cans was like standing in a dark room trying to work out where the light switch was. The only conclusion I could come to was that they had worked loose in the current and floated away in some cruel repayment for something I had done in the past.

So, I did what any level headed calm relaxed fisherman would do - I went looking for the beer. I knew it was a long-shot but there was the slim possibility that they had got caught up on that tree I was looking at further downstream. Copper coloured leaves were draping into the water and, with a bit of celestial help, the beer may just have got caught up there.

Working my way downstream I scanned the water, the rocks and the reeds fringing the river like a hit-man trying to locate his target. The water got deeper as I got closer. The rocks up here are very slippery and I have seen more than one person go over, so I only went so far before crouching down to get a better look under the branches. As I did so, I saw a glint to my left, but it wasn't what I was looking for. It was a grayling, a nice one too. She had risen through the quick current to nip something off the surface. I stopped looking for the beer and started looking for fish. Up she came again. I marked the spot and retreated for the rod.

Wading back into position, I bit the Grey Wulff off the tippet and replaced it with a size 14 Klinkhammer from my hat. It had nothing to do with an understanding of entomology - it was just that I could see it better in the poor light under the trees. It took a while to pin point her but then up she came again and I followed her back down. She had risen with speed but there didn't seem any hurry - like a swallow taking a midge in mid-flight on a balmy summer's day.

The water had that clarity that autumn can bring and although I couldn't see the grayling I could see her shadow dancing over the gravel. The kiss of a dimple drifting downstream confirmed her location. As I made the cast, everything turned to slow motion, the buzzards hung mid-flight, the reeds stopped crackling and the grazing sheep looked my way as if something important was about to happen. It did. As soon as the fly touched down the grayling nailed it. I didn't strike, the line just tightened and she was on. She fought like most grayling do, solid little dashes in between hanging in the current, using her dorsal as a brake until I glided her to hand. Colours bounced off her scales like a mirror ball. She felt strong as she shuddered and hoisted that great sail of hers. There was an amber tinge to the fish from the reflected autumn leaves. I remember thinking it was a similar colour to how that glass of beer would have looked. I marvelled at that fish for longer than was necessary. I held her up, savouring the moment, quenching my thirst before popping her back. As I did so, those colours turned to camouflage as she evaporated.

I fished on without success, doing a lot of walking in the process, until the sun dropped back behind the hills, the sparkle went from the water and the temperature dropped to how it had felt when I had arrived eight hours before. As I made my way back to the car I had to be content with a single grayling and two little trout for my efforts. I cut through the woods, over a deceptively steep slope and stopped to see if the otter was still fishing. He wasn't.

Two boys appeared, about twelve to thirteen years old I guessed. One was wearing a cloth cap at a jaunty angle. The other was whacking crusty cow pats with a stick like a practising golfer.

'You boys didn't happen to see a couple of cans of beer floating down river did you?' I asked.

'Seen them, drunk them!' Came the reply.

They speeded up and choked back the giggles. I stood there, stunned, as I watched the boys vault the gate and skip down the little lane. The taller one tossed something into the air and smacked it, two handed, over the fence with the resounding crack of willow on aluminium. If it hadn't been for the aerodynamics of an empty beer can it would have been a clear six. They turned and grinned, making their run before the fielder could get to them.

Back down by the river, where I had caught that grayling, I noticed some footprints in the mud. They were about the same size as the wellingtons the young Butch Cassidy and Sundance Kid had been wearing. Technically, this was theft and I was looking at the crime scene, but I had to allow myself a smile. I would have done the same if I were lucky enough to be 13 years old and some dumb fisherman had left his beer for all to see. Let's face it, boys tend to regard these things as 'finders keepers' rather than a brutal, wanton criminal act that may leave the innocent victim needing stress counselling for the rest of the fishing season. But, even if I had been able to catch them, maybe I should have thanked them. After all, if I hadn't gone looking for the missing beer, I wouldn't have caught that fish.

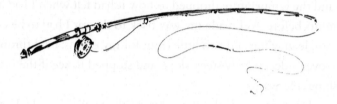

STONES

WORKING IT OUT - THE RIVER WYE

*When you haven't caught a fish for several weeks you have
to ask yourself questions - like, 'Why am I doing this?'*

It was morning. Very early. A mist hung over the water. Although it was summer there was an uncertainty in the temperature that couldn't decide whether to let the rising sun warm up the land or the water cool it down. It was nice and quiet.

I was setting up the rod whilst looking at the river and most other things that caught my attention. A dew glistened on the grass. The rabbits looked a little nervous. A fox skulking along a hedgerow explained their concern and the fox, in turn, looked at me and decided that this might be a good time to get out of the way herself. It was a calming atmosphere and when a woodpecker hammered out the dawn I cleaned the polaroids on my shirt cuff and went looking for a fish. The timing seemed about right.

As the light increased, the mist evaporated and the river took on that nice smooth look that has you saying, 'Perfect.' The water was clear with that tinge of emerald that excites fish and fishermen alike. Around the next bend in the river there is a high bank where you can gaze down into Nature's aquarium allowing you to see just what is (or isn't) down there. It's a great place, except for one thing - the fish can see you too.

Crawling up on places like this is always exciting. If you can keep low, avoid sinking your elbows into a fresh cow pat and not flinch too much when a thistle slaps you on the cheek, then you stand a chance of seeing those fish you've been looking for. Sometimes they're there, sometimes they're not. If they are not, then it is usually because you've made a clumsy approach. On this morning they were, so a little self-congratulation was allowed.

There were three small barbel tucked up against a sunken tree trunk. They were grouped so closely that they were touching each other as if they were getting warmed up on a cold morning. Several juvenile grayling flitted about where the water shallowed up. A metropolis of minnows stretching several yards wafted upriver like smoke from a camp fire. There was a chub down there too, holding her position just in front of the sunken tree. Her head swayed from side to side, her fins worked the current, her body was quivering like a cat about to pounce on a mouse. She was hungry.

I cast a very small piece of luncheon meat over her head. I used the smallest lead I possessed and cast it well upstream but she still sensed it going in. I waited until she settled down, then I waited even longer to make sure and then I nudged the bait down - very slowly. When it settled about five feet in front of her, she picked up the scent, glided forward, opened her big white mouth and then turned and bolted back downstream in total panic upsetting the young barbel as she went and dispersing the minnows like a sparrow hawk splitting a flock of starlings. The speed they moved made me realise that, if these tiny fish grew to over a pound in weight, they would probably be the most sought after sporting fish in the world.

It had taken over an hour for me to make that first cast and I messed it up in less time than it took for those minnows to get out of the way. I honestly couldn't work it out. As far as I could see I had done everything right. I had been quiet, kept off the skyline, fished as light as possible and still I messed it up. When you keep on messing things up you have to question why? There is not a great deal else you can do.

That chub couldn't have seen the hook (that was buried in the tiny bait on the end of a very long hook length) and it wasn't the line because that entered the water at an angle that kept it well out of her way. I came to the only conclusion I could and that was that the chub had been panicked by the lead, not the casting in, but the static lead itself. And, as I said, it was a pretty small one too. Was this a visual thing? A smell thing? I didn't know. I still don't know, but she certainly didn't like that lead.

There was no point continuing to fish where I was because every fish within fifty yards was on edge at the chub's panic in just the same way as you would lose interest in eating your Aromatic Crispy Duck if the chef ran through the Cantonese restaurant shouting 'Fire!'

I couldn't get into the fishing elsewhere because I kept thinking that if that lead had spooked that particular chub then it would have a similar effect on any other fish I was after. Now, even I know that we have all caught fish using leads, that's exactly how the majority of them are caught on this water. But when I get something into my head like this I tend to scratch it. So I moved on to save me the embarrassment of looking into an empty river to do a bit of that scratching.

It was whilst I was sat down by a gravel run further downstream that I picked up one of the pebbles that were cutting into my buttocks. I turned it over in my fingers, tossed it up and down in the palm of my hand and compared its size and weight to that little lead I had been using. It was one of those light bulb moments you see in the Tom and Jerry cartoons. The lead came off the line and the stone went on. That sounds a lot easier than it was. It wasn't easy at all. I spent a good couple of hours messing around trying to tie the damn thing on. Tried doing it with fishing line, an elastic band, a bit of cotton cut from my shirt sleeve, even tried moulding clay around the swivel. After several stones had flown off at dangerous angles every time I made a gentle cast, I made the hike back to the car, super-glued a link of line on to the stone and tied the line on to the main line. The glue took longer to set than it said on the side of the tube, but it worked.

Back by the river I lowered the stone into the shallows to see how it looked. It looked so good I couldn't see it. I reckoned I had just done something special. All I had to do now was catch a fish to prove just how clever a boy I was. Seeing as how the only fish I had spotted that morning were those off the high bank that's where I went.

The chub was back at her station, the barbel were less tolerant but those minnows had returned to commuting to wherever they commute to. I made the same cast, from the same position, using the same sized bait. That chub made the same approach. This time she just picked up the bait without hesitation, wheeled round and let the current glide her back downstream. I pinned her with a clinical efficiency that she didn't deserve. It was one of the best mornings fishing I've ever had.

This happened several years ago and I have refined the use of stones quite a bit since then and I'm enjoying my fishing again. Using them appeals to me immensely. I like the idea that it works. I like the feeling that you no longer have to walk around with pockets full of lead and the fact that you can pick up the stones as you go. I like the simplicity. I like the fact that you no longer have to queue up in the local tackle shop on a Friday lunchtime to replace all the expensive lead you lost the previous weekend. I also like the fact that stones taken from the river don't pollute it. They can be a really good solution to a tricky fishy problem but there are still times when a lead will out-fish a stone. I don't really like to admit it up front but it's true. I still use rolling bullet leads because I haven't managed to drill a small hole right the way through a spherical stone - yet! Still, if I arrive without any leads it no longer worries me. In clear water conditions (over gravel or in amongst weed) I go for a stone every time.

I'm not the first person to have used stones instead of leads and I won't be the last. But at least I did work it out for myself on that morning and that's something that gives me a certain sense of satisfaction. I also now realise that there is a lot more to it than simply replacing that shop bought lead with a stone. There are flat stones, long stones, round stones and all have their place. I've tried most of them. Swivels, bits of line and tubing all have their uses and I'm reasonably proud of some of the stones I've made up by the edge of the river. They may not look that poetic dangling from an eleven foot fishing rod but they look beautifully functional in the water.

I know people who spend hours making traditional quill floats that are things of beauty, people who stoop over a fly tying vice to emerge hours later with a mayfly imitation that looks more like a mayfly than a mayfly. People who can do this deserve more recognition in art terms than a Turner Prize winner but a stone, at the end of the day, is a stone, and that's the beauty. It's so simple, it's obvious.

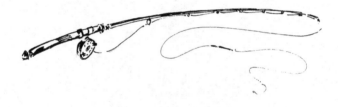

BREAK A LEG

POLITICS - THE TACKLE SHOP

*There have been some terrible decisions made
relating to fishing. The most catastrophic was the
abolition of the coarse fishing closed season.*

Talk of abolition echoed around the tackle shop. Politics polluted what
had always been a quiet haven; the place that I visited when I needed
to waste some cash, or to get out of the rain, had turned into a debating
chamber. Like all arguments, both sides thought they were right. There
wasn't that much any of us could do about it even though some of us
tried. Opinions are dearly held and besides, money was involved.

I just happened to be standing in the D&J Fishing Store, Cirencester,
eyeing up a rather expensive fishing reel that I didn't need, when an old
boy I knew came in for some trout flies. The 'discussion' by the counter
(which by now had disintegrated to the pointed fingers stage) made him
a little nervous. Not wishing to get involved in someone else's fight, he
whispered, 'What's it all about?' As he did so he looked down through
his bifocal spectacles and selected half a dozen Blue Winged Olives.

'They want to ban the closed season.' I said.

He paused, then replied.

'Stupid bastards!'

It was said louder than he usually speaks. He didn't look up, he just tipped
the flies back into the old wooden tray and walked out. His statement
was short and absolutely correct. Like myself, he knew that banning the
close season would be catastrophic, although it was healthier not to have
said so at that particular moment in time.

Coarse fishing, to my knowledge, has always had a closed season and if it hasn't then it should have had. In this respect fishing was similar to other sports – we have a cricket season, a football season and seasons for all sorts of things. Then it was decided, 'Hey! Wouldn't it be nice to fish all year round?' When the possibility of 'extending' the season got aired you either agreed or disagreed. I disagreed, but then everybody I knew said, 'Well you would, wouldn't you!'

There was confusion. Average mild mannered fishing folk turned into politicians as they became experts on the spawning habits of our native fish species in an attempt to enforce their side of the debate. It was all very complicated but if you dug down to the bottom of the argument for the abolition it was this:– 'If I want to go fishing every day of the year, who the hell are you to stop me!'

The vast majority (we were told) demanded the right to fish all year round. They dismissed any consequences and, like a particular bully I remember at school, they got their own way by force rather than reasoning. There wasn't much you could do without getting severely hurt extremely quickly. Perhaps they would think about what they had done in a few years from that day but I doubted it. Furthermore, when they began to moan about littered fisheries with stunted fish (which they have) it wasn't their fault either, was it?

A new breed of angler had evolved and, like the Thatcher child he was, he wanted everything, immediately. He was competitive, loud and aggressive in his attempts to become the best. He craved success whilst I have never understood what success means in fishing terms. Big business made him fashionable and the same big business sponsored the abolition because, on paper, they stood to increase turnover by 25% – 'Why sell to people nine months of the year when you can sell to them for twelve?' I continued to disagree.

I wrote a few letters, did my share of moaning and started on a T-shirt design that was going to read, 'Don't mess with my fishing!' I dropped that one on the grounds that it didn't have the right tone of voice for what I was trying to protect but it would have made me feel better if I had worn it.

I lost. Lakes are now open every day of the year. Holes have been dug, fish chucked in, trees hacked down, paths cemented, toilets erected and everything spruced up for convenience fishing that also costs more than you're used to paying. Rivers survived the onslaught - just - but, even after all those years have past, I can see the next bit of reasoning right around the corner - 'We have been able to fish the lakes all year round for ages now, why not the rivers?'

The 'old' closed season was there to give spawning fish a bit of peace and quiet while they went through the important things in life. I am aware that not all fish spawn in this period but a large percentage do. The closed season also allowed the banks of the pools and gravel pits to rejuvenate themselves through the spring. All in all, our waters were a great deal healthier for the break. Sure, it would have been nice to go coarse fishing but you do have to protect what you are fishing for in the first place and the anticipation of a new season compensated for the lack of bent fishing rods and its disappearance remains a great shame.

The opening night of the season was always special and, like the opening night of a theatre production, everybody wished everybody else the best of luck. The 16th of June had every coarse fisherman on edge. We thought about it for weeks in advance and when the day arrived it was a celebration. The only bad thing was that it didn't rank highly in the solitude stakes, but when you haven't threaded worm on a hook for three months you can put up with that.

I remember, with affection, fishing one particular opening night with my friend Rodney in the Lea Valley. For weeks before the event our minds swirled with images of sweet scented dawns and olive flanked tench because that's what early season fishing is all about. June and tench fishing are inseparable, they are made for each other. Both are so perfect and when in the presence of beauty it is necessary to take the time to look at it. Tench are fabulous creatures. They look and feel like shimmering velvet, a perfect cut of marble with rubies for eyes, and they remind me of why poets put pen to paper.

The planning for the new season was going well. Then I broke my foot in a pub. I won't go into how because nobody I have told actually believes what really happened. My own mother went so far as to say that if an accident was to happen to me it was bound to be in a pub. I looked for sympathy but all I got was a trip to Whipps Cross hospital where I was loaded down with a large plaster cast, instructions to come back in ten weeks (unless it started to *really* hurt), and none of that sympathy. Plans for the opening night disintegrated like a fractured rod and then panic set in. How could I fish with my leg in plaster? How could I carry my rod when I couldn't walk without crutches? How, even if I could resolve these minor obstacles, could I get to the water's edge? My fishing partner couldn't drive!

I told the doctor (who looked like one of those anti-fishing types) that the plaster would have to come off before an exotic holiday in June that I had already booked. He said, 'Cancel the holiday.' He then went on to attend some lesser hurt individual who had just been wheeled in after a major road accident.

The pool we had planned to fish had me now. I couldn't get her image out of my mind. Then I made the mistake of hobbling to work where I found myself in the ridiculous situation where I could go to where I didn't want to, but couldn't go to where I did want to! I began to reply aggressively whenever some suited office worker asked, 'Been skiing then?'

A man who fishes can only take so much of this pressure, so I snapped and chipped off enough of the plaster cast with a ball-hammer to enable me to feel the clutch peddle with my toes. A little dangerous?

Perhaps. Irresponsible? Certainly. But there was no way I was missing an opening night, they were that important. When people tell me that I must be mad to go fishing I sometimes think they may be right.

It was what could be called 'an interesting drive' yet, as the car lurched to a halt, I began to unwind before looking at the real obstacle ahead of me. It took some taking in. The pool lay half a mile away over rough ground. My hands were bound up to cut down the blisters, crutches were thrust under armpits and Rodney had to struggle with all that tackle, which served him right for never having learned to drive.

We forced our way through the undergrowth whilst untangling rods, nets and crutches at a time that has you wondering, 'Why am I doing this?' Then the answer came. Once through the jungle we were greeted by the calm of water and a marvelously overgrown wilderness hidden in the North London suburbs. The wait had been rewarded once again.

Rodney tied back the branches so we could get a cast in, dragged out a slender channel in the weed, put in the bait, took the rods out of hibernation and made ready for that magical first cast at midnight. I put my foot up, closed my eyes and waited.

That traditional first cast at midnight hooked up on the tree to my right. Rodney's did a similar thing to the left, but when our unpracticed hands had resolved the casting problems we settled down to the mesmerizing task of staying awake whilst staring at floats that glow in the dark. During the first hour the expectancy makes this possible – just. Then the haunting hours take over and play tricks with your eyes. The float danced from side to side in the still water. It levitated from the surface in the most convincing manner before disappearing as if somebody had switched off the light. Any attempt to strike contacted with absolutely nothing and the whole procedure of renewing soft bread baits and avoiding trees in the dark was repeated. But the reward came as my float moved in the same way that my imagination had seen numerous times that night and then disappeared below the surface as if cork had turned to stone. The old feelings burst back as the rod jerked into the first tench of the season – it was electrifying.

First this way, then the other. The rod tip cushions the unseen movements of the fish as it careers its way through weed and underwater corridors, opening the throttle as if joining an empty motorway. Every turn and jolt was transmitted through the slender rod. The fish was in the driving seat from the off. Eventually I gained control and then, almost too soon, it's over. The luxury of torch light is abandoned and the natural glow of the moon shimmers over the flank of the flagging fish. The net is eased forward, the tension is relaxed from the line, the rod straightens and the prize is yours.

This is what it always used to be like. That first fish was always the same – so magnificent, so rewarding. Belief in tradition was always fulfilled. The three months abstinence had been worthwhile because without the closed season there is no 16th of June and fishing without the 16th of June just doesn't seem right. That night was so delicious that it needed repeating. Sadly, I can't repeat the process because the amateur politicians in the tackle shops, and the sponsors that encouraged them, have taken it away.

Stupid bastards.

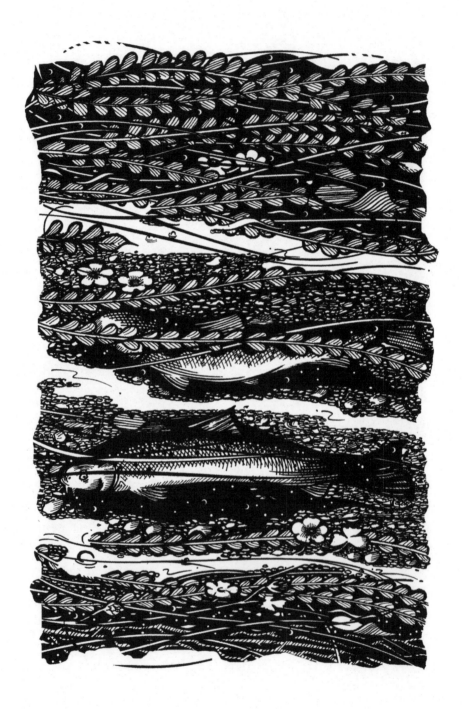

NATURE'S NARCOTIC

LOSING A FISH - THE RIVER LUGG

*A morning on the river led me to the conclusion
that you can spend a long time messing things up.*

I've been walking the river since dawn. I've thrown a bait here and there
in all the likely looking places and a few in those I hadn't noticed before.
Having spooked a good fish earlier, I begin to wonder if it would have
been more productive to have stayed in one place, to have persevered, but
that's not really my style of fishing. A little doubt about prospects creeps
in and I tell myself that the light is getting far too bright for the fish
to remain in the shallows. Nevertheless, I keep walking, keep looking,
there's a little fishing in between, but not much.

The river, just being by the river, keeps the disappointment of the
missed opportunity in check. The lack of fish is not catastrophic, that
is how it goes sometimes, and I am content because I've seen more
kingfishers than people. Even so, sometimes when you are alone, the
landscape becomes so vast it closes in when it should be expanding
out. With so many options in front of you and so much freedom, the
expanse that refuses to fit into the viewfinder of the Nikon can become
claustrophobic - no matter how wide-angled the lens.

The sun has now peeped over the hill and is spilling it's warmth into
the valley. The thick woollen shirt that was the first thing I put on is now
the first thing I take off. A comfort has become an inconvenience and it
is tied around my waist which makes me cooler but makes the walking
harder. There's a lot of walking to do too, so I have trimmed everything

down as much as possible – a rod, reel, net and a bag of bait. The end result is that I am travelling pretty light. It is a liberating sensation. When you realise you've been carrying a tackle bag about most weekends of your life without opening it up, it's a good idea to leave it behind and stick the hooks in your top pocket.

The walk back along the river seems longer than it did on the way up. The prospect of a break has crept into my head but I trudge on, looking for a fish or a good place to have a rest. Nature has a way of squaring up to laziness. Coming across a bend in the river (where the current undercuts the near bank) it hits me right on the chin. It was a good punch too.

I had seen the spot in the early morning but it didn't hold too much interest then. Now it feels as if this is the only place in the Universe. It's not a dramatically physical transformation, not even a poetic metamorphism, just a feeling. A weird feeling. I'm uncertain why I've got it, but it is a good feeling.

The sun has now burnt the remaining clouds away and light is bouncing off the water like a car's headlights off a wet road. It makes the shade offered by an overhanging tree appealing, a place for fish and fishermen to rest. The change in light allows me to see a patch of gravel that I hadn't realised existed. It's exciting, but it also allows me to see that there aren't any fish down there either. Logic and theory have little pull here, so I remain still. Looking. Wondering. Praying. It is all very pleasant and I have just cut to the core of what this is all about. There is no rush. It doesn't matter – but it does really.

My fishing rod rests against the tree giving a focus to the panorama of the valley. It is a beautiful image. Fishing is art.

I keep looking, crouch down further as my eyes adjust to the darker water and my mind clears itself to take it in. Mobile telephones, deadlines, appointments, prestige, yellow post-it-notes, 'I've done this,' and, 'I've got that,' have been left at the office. Work has left my head and the river is sweeping through the void, flushing out the crap and refreshing it with thoughts that rank highly in the photo album of my memory along with similar days and family.

The shade of the tree has prevented the sun from drying out the dew, so I end up with patches on my elbows that remind me of a particular teacher at primary school. Despite the flashback, my concentration is on the water. When it gets acclimatised it's through the water.

Peering into the depths, with the hat brim pulled down like the film stars wear them and with hands shielding eyes from the water's reflection, I have slipped into my inner world. It's like looking through the kaleidoscope of youth and it feels as if this is what I was born to do.

Initially, I see only stones, pebbles, drifting leaves and strands of weed. Once I have remembered to forget what is always there and I search for what *isn't* always there, my vision blinks into perspective like the frosty image that pops back into focus at a slide show. What I am looking for isn't on the river bed, it isn't a foot above it, it is somewhere, very precisely, in-between. I go through the pointless exercise of trying to see if I can get a better view without the polaroids. I can't. So they are slipped back on. Trying to re-focus through the surface is like trying to recognise a stranger through a stained glass window – difficult – but possible. Anything is possible when you've got this feeling.

Then I see it. A fish. After a while more materialise from the void and I slither backwards to get the bait. I feel ten years old again – I've got the buzz and my hands are trembling.

Looking at a bag of worms and an open can of sweet corn, I opt for the corn. More visible. Try and get them feeding. Get a clearer look at them. Work out their pecking order. Pick out the pretty fish. This is labelled as reasoning. It strongly resembles panic. I'm on overdrive.

I wriggle back (commando style) and test the current with a grain of corn. The pace of the river looks slow but the corn sails past mid-water. The offering is dismissed like a piece of ash, flicked off a Cuban cigar.

The river flushes it towards the sea as the excitement staples me to the ground.

There's this sort of automatic-underarm-panic-backhand-of-a-toss as an enthusiastic fistful of bait arcs across the skyline peppering the surface several yards upstream. As soon as it leaves my hand, I cringe at my foolishness. Too much! It's going to land in the wrong place. It doesn't. I have judged the river without even thinking about it and it all seems gloriously ridiculous as the corn settles on the visible gravel patch and cascades, nice... and... slowly... under... the... tree. Beautiful.

After a while, there's a flash, five, maybe six foot down, which slaps me back to reality. I can't really see her, just a brilliant spark as she turns broadside. This is no minnow. This is what it is all about.

There's another flash.

I am pretty certain that they are barbel down there yet I still question my judgement. The light is good, but not great. At that size, the only other thing it could be is a salmon and if it is, she's developed a strange liking for feeding heavily on food that she shouldn't be eating and at a time when Nature dictates she wouldn't. Whatever it is, I want it. Legal, illegal, ethical or not. I want it real bad.

There is another blinding flash and now I know it's a barbel.

I belt out another fistful of bait.

'Why the hell did I do that?'

Think... take it easy... 'Jesus, give me the rod, NOW!'

I attempt to slow down by looking upstream searching for somebody to witness what I know is about to happen. The only audience I have are cattle and (although every single one of them is looking at me) they don't seem that impressed, they just carry on chewing. Time is taken to change the size of the hook, to crimp down the barb, to check the knot that fixes it to the line, the line itself and the reel that holds the line. My mind is bulging with expectation and it is beginning to hurt.

It has now been twenty minutes since the buzz stopped me. Now I take it head on. The closer I get to the river, the more intense it becomes. There's a worry about any shadow the rod will cast on the water. The hook is loaded with a single grain of corn. It takes two attempts to get this right. I am at the mercy of a powerful drug. I'm on a high and reacting at a faster pace than I'm used to. At this stage, I could walk on water but that would spook the fish and there's nobody else about to witness the miracle in the first place.

The pickup arm on the reel is opened, the flick out judged, the line mended back upstream, and the beads of lead flutter the bait down towards the gods. The grain of corn falls short into the sunlit gravel and I leave it there for a while, too scared to correct the mistake. The last thing I want to do is make another cast. It's gamble time.

Line is taken up and the lead given a little nudge to lift it out of the bright spot. The current trundles it in to the shade as I feel the river bed drop into a very attractive depression. The reel engages itself and the clunk it makes, makes me cringe. This is what it's all about. This is what I would like to show all those people who keep asking, 'Why do you go fishing anyway?' - this is proper fishing.

Anticipation jerks time. I savour the seconds, whilst wishing they'd hurry up. Suddenly the line vibrates, tightens and I feel a tiny tug. The reaction is automatic. The hook is set. The rod bucks. There's a slap on the end of the line. I roll over on to my side to get a better angle, both hands clamped onto the rod to take up the strain in an attempt to get the fish away from the sunken tree roots. The rod tip lunges down to the surface of the water, dangerously low, the line creaks through the rod rings, the reel's trying to give line, my left hand is trying to stop it and the buzz is roaring around an ancient vale in a cry of victory.

I attempt to get up onto one knee to get a better angle. The rod kicks, then straightens. The line goes limp. The lead beads catapult embarrassingly upstream and I curse in a way that makes Lucifer blush.

As I manage to stand up, the rod lies on the ground but I don't remember dropping it and I lift up my arms in some primeval display of, 'I just don't believe that.' As I shake my head, the cattle lower theirs in sympathy and return to their grazing.

There is no point trying again, those fish are now well aware of what I was trying to do, but I keep looking at the water in disbelief. It's exactly as it was a minute earlier except for two things. No fish. No buzz. With every high, there's a low. Knowing doesn't help.

Trying to be practical, I check the hook. There's nothing wrong there. I stand still for a while, angry at myself, ashamed, like the little boy who keeps saying 'Sorry' for something when he doesn't know what he's supposed to have done in the first place.

Eventually I walk away from the disaster zone, dragging the rod behind me. I find it hard to look at the river. It is like walking away from your first ever girl friend. There's only one person who has messed this up because there's only one person here. I am not annoyed with the river, I'm annoyed with myself. There is no excuse for a lost fish. None. Ever.

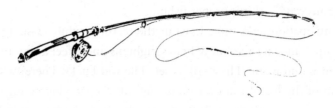

SPAGHETTI INCIDENT

TENCH & CARP - GLOUCESTERSHIRE

*Having moved from London I had to find
somewhere to live, some work and, most
importantly, somewhere to fish.*

I was standing, thigh deep, in cool, muddy water and I was enjoying it. The patch of water I was wallowing in belonged to one of the series of gravel pits that orbit South Cerney in Gloucestershire. This place was not what I was used to, not what I was really looking for, yet it held some good fish and it was those fish that attracted me. The place also happened to attract a lot of other people with swimming costumes, windsurf boards and, of course, fishing rods. So, I found the most inaccessible place at the far end in a little reed fringed bay and pinned my hopes there.

As long as I was careful only to fish those areas that appeared un-fishable and kept the bank in such a state that it looked to other curious anglers that 'nobody in their right mind would fish here,' then I could get the solitude that is so conducive to good fishing. This was why I was standing up to my thighs in the water rather than leaving footprints and flattening the perfectly comfortable grass bank. Cocooned in the corner I could forget the remaining 147 acres of windswept gravel pit and pretend I was fishing some exclusive estate lake far away from civilisation. It was a great thought but I was not alone. The gravel pit was quite heavily fished yet most avoided this area because the bay not only sheltered the water it sheltered an Armada of small yachts whose masts rattled and clanged in varying degrees depending on how strong the breeze blew.

Tucked away amongst the reeds, I grew to find the sound comforting. One particular boat was a lovely old thing, all wood and thick green paint that, on a warm day, you could smell from fifty yards. Early Sunday morning, 10 o'clock prompt, two elderly pirates rowed out their yellow dingy and boarded the mother ship without the distraction of conversation. The deep red canvas sail was hoisted and off they went playing Swallows and Amazons of their youth before returning, exactly two hours later, to the sailing club bar that opened at precisely 12 o'clock in a splendid display of nautical punctuality.

Whatever the prevailing weather conditions, these mariners managed to drop anchor, paddle ashore and adjust their ties just as the latch on the club house clicked in an upward position. I was never allowed in the hallowed club house but I reckon that these characters had their names etched on little brass plaques on respective bar stools and didn't have to tell the barman what they wanted to drink. Probably didn't say much to each other either. I imagine there was no need.

General opinion among other anglers was that the fish would be scared by the boats. The web of ropes, chains and anchors was considered another risk. I thought that they were getting a bit paranoid about, what looked to me, the most attractive place to fish.

Having found the place, I persevered with pinches of bread, swan mussels and worms. As I grew familiar with the behavior of the fish, I noticed that they spent their days under the shade the boats provided and in amongst the security of the ropes and anchor chains but they travelled, early morning and every evening, to feast in the margins. I started to catch enough to make crawling out of bed worthwhile. I was enjoying myself, it was nice and leisurely but I was putting a lot of thought in to it so, when I caught a few fish, and, as I started to refine the tackle, and to get the balance just right I felt at ease with the water and I caught a few more.

Then, one morning things didn't go as planned. Those fish didn't show. Something had changed.

I had waded out and was waiting for the tench to arrive. They were late and I began to wonder what had changed. Then it happened.

A dead branch snapped behind me and split the silence.

'Jesus Christ.' – I span around as quickly as waders allow. Panic stopped me from dropping my rod. Behind luminous reeds hovered an immense green monster. A crick in my neck jabbed paralysis through my body, mud sucked at my feet, gravity became very obvious – I was going down. My vision was transfixed on two black reflective eyes a good two and a half inches in diameter – they were fixed on me. It was impossible to look away. Tight green skin encased an apparent skull, a mouth twitched, then gaped, revealing a hideous grin. Two giant tentacles rose from behind the reeds. One clasped a huge steaming enamel drinking vessel, the other a chocolate digestive biscuit – it was a carp angler.

'Cup of tea?' it squawked.

An unusual contact had been made and I sloshed ashore to regain my composure. Hitting dry land, sea legs gave way as I beached myself and flipped off my hat. It peeled back it's skin in sinister slow motion to reveal a human face underneath his quilted (I can sleep anywhere) survival suit. I looked for bad weather rolling in over the horizon – I can't say that I saw any. His fishing partner, who was dressed identically, joined us and we passed the time by sitting on the grass, looking out over misty water and chatting. After the tea, I wandered around to their pitch which was cunningly hidden from sight in a dense clump of hawthorn bushes some thirty yards around the bay.

'Clever.' I thought. 'Very clever.'

The illusion of some alien from outer space would have been confirmed earlier if I had seen all the electronic gadgetry clipped onto their fishing rods. Two green capsules sprouted three fishing rods apiece.

They, in turn, rested on an assortment of expensive looking stainless steel tripods that would not have looked out of place in the New York Museum of Modern Art. I had never seen so much pristine tackle at such close range without a price tag on it. All of their equipment had been pinned, very precisely, into the ground with a heavy mallet that lay by the camp entrance. This, at least, explained why the fish had not arrived that morning.

They happened to mention they hadn't caught any carp during the night and I told them that I had failed to land any tench. Which made us pretty equal if you count these sort of things. I never did discover their names and if I did, I have forgotten them, but we began to hold each other with a mutual respect. We were doing the same thing, we just happened to be doing it in totally different ways.

They had decided upon a season-long campaign to catch one of the few carp that inhabited the water. The size of these creatures was measured on an escalating scale of rumour and folklore. Few had been seen, fewer hooked, none, to my knowledge, ever landed. I envied the quest, admired the dedication, but I couldn't quite warm to the military precision.

As the weekends unrolled, I would often be joined by the two characters as they sat and watched my float with as much hope that it would go under as I had. I would have been equally excited, probably more so, if they had hooked their Goliath.

I was lazy - they did all the work. The initial cup of tea on the first meeting was accompanied by a bacon sandwich on the second that I could smell as it hit the frying pan. I started supplying cold beer as lunchtimes approached and I obviously impressed, for on the next visit, after I was allowed the privilege of a little fishing, a familiar rustling of reeds was accompanied by - 'Cup of tea and full English breakfast?'

Even though our paths only crossed once a week, things were getting out of hand. I began looking after their expensive tackle whilst they popped to the pub. They primed my swim with ground bait on Friday evenings and I appeared with the luxury of fresh milk for the early morning tea on Saturday. Usually, I go to great lengths to avoid other people when I untie the cloth bag that houses the fishing rod but now I found it hard to fish anywhere else. Even if the fishing wasn't that spectacular, the hospitality most certainly was. The reeds fringing the water were suffering from the increasing ferrying of, 'Better this offering if you can.' The original camouflage of the hawthorn bushes resembled saloon style kitchen swing doors of a popular American style steak house. They never caught their carp, they didn't even have a sniff, but they sure knew how to eat.

As the season progressed, the tench became finicky and were only interested in grazing over small items of food. A single grain of sweet corn would have been a good choice but I had agreed with the carp boys (under a bit of pressure) not to use that bait because, they theorised, it would spook the carp. I reckoned they were talking crap but, all the same, I complied so as not to smash their ambitions. I used casters instead.

To fish these smaller baits, you need to scale everything down to match the size of food the fish are feeding on. The combination of thin line, weedy water, small hook and powerful fish is dangerous fishing. Exciting fishing. I like it.

One morning the yachts fell silent as the breeze exhausted itself and the air became warm and sticky. The water took on an inviting inky blackness that pond skaters like to dash about on.

A yawning sun highlighted pin-prick bubbles hinting at interest beneath the void. The carp boys watched as I flicked out the float and I watched as the float cocked itself upright, nice... and... slowly.

The tench arrived on cue and there were more to come, I could see them rolling on the surface as they made their way from the boats to their feeding ground. The water clouded up with competition for the free breakfast. Tiny fragments of waterlogged reeds popped to the surface in the most encouraging display of greed I've witnessed.

Initially I got only tiny frustrating indications on my float so I swapped the float for a thinner version and scaled down the size of the hook. As a result I started to get what every tench fisher dreams of – good, positive bites that made the float lift, quiver and then slide away only to be jerked back as the strike is made and the fish is nailed.

'Splendid sport, Peter.' I said.

Neither of my spectators were called Peter, nor understood what I meant, but then neither had been taught by Mr. Crabtree – they were too young.

I made the best display of bending rods, screeching reels and splashing fish as I could – well, why not? Every indication transformed itself into a fish. The rod catapulted over as the thump, thump, thump of a tench created one of the most pleasant sounds known to mankind – the purring of a carefully set clutch accompanied by the backing vocals of stretched line as fish after fish were encouraged towards the waiting net. I was in my element. I had become a celebrity and I was making the most of it.

The inevitable happened. One of my fan club decided I'd had enough enjoyment for one individual and summoned up enough cheek to ask if he could have a go. As we swapped places, I handed him the rod as if it were an autograph.

To jeers from the gallery he missed several sail away bites. Then his reward came as one was hooked and I worried about the slender tip of my rod as he hauled the creature towards the net. He was not used to such delicate tackle. I think he'd forgotten this simple fact and must have thought he was connected to his carp, with his 12lb. line and his broom handle of a rod. Incredibly, everything held. 'Bloody easy this tench fishing,' came the cry as a dripping net was dangled in my face.

Out went the float once more and out it came again as a bite was missed. A bush, a good four yards away, claimed the float and line in one of the most mathematically complicated tangles I've seen. By the time I had reset the whole affair, the tench had either finished their feast or had been scared away by the commotion. Probably the latter. Breakfast was late that morning.

I never repeated the performance because the carp boys announced that they were 'Pulling off the water after next weekend.' They had fished the summer through without a single nibble from their carp.

A grand finale was needed and Friday evening at home supplied an idea that catapulted me back to childhood pranks. Clearing away the debris of my cooking, I realised how easy it would be to re-heat the remaining bolognese sauce and boil some fresh pasta by the edge of the water.

In the morning, off I trudged - fishing rod, landing net, stove, saucepan, pasta, salad, pesto sauce, forks, plates, a tray and a side dish of wilting salad that I stored in an old margarine tub.

Arriving a little later than usual, I was lucky enough to catch one or two tench before they moved on. During the afternoon I left my companions behind and went to buy some Parmesan cheese from the village store.

All was quiet when I got back. Next door were asleep. Again.

At 6.30 precisely the cooking commenced. It was pretty basic stuff too. Having forgotten the colander, draining the pasta became as difficult as keeping the midges away but I got there in the end.

I picked my way through the reeds trying to be as quiet as a young Sioux buck, whilst attempting to carry plates of spaghetti, forks and salad with an almost white T-shirt draped over my left arm for maximum effect. Parting the bush on entrance to their encampment gave me the opportunity to release my carefully rehearsed lines.

'Spaghetti bolognese for three, Sir?'

'Why certainly,' came the reply.

As they stirred from their sleeping bags, I sensed something dramatic was about to happen. One of them lent over to their cooking area in the most irritatingly casual manner, flipped out a hot length of cooking foil and inquired with the same beaming smile as on that first meeting – 'Garlic bread?'

A few weeks after the carp anglers had left (whilst I was fishing for tench with a small hook and a single grain of sweet corn) I hooked their carp very close to the margins. It was a leather carp and I don't think she even knew she was hooked. She rose to the surface, before rolling over my line, breaking it as if it were a spider's web. I could guess at the size of that fish but you wouldn't believe me if I told you.

PHIL HUMM

A FISHING PARTNER

*A good fishing partner is one who is quite happy to
break down the rod and head for the pub around
about the same time you do.*

When you spend a large amount of your spare time by the edge of
water you see some remarkable things. I have watched a pike snatch two
ducklings off the surface of a gravel pit, seen a swimming squirrel, a man
coming down the middle of the river Wye on a bicycle, a buzzard pick
a lamprey from the edge of the water and then watched as it struggled
in an unsuccessful attempt to fly away with its awkward and downright
ugly prize. Once I had the pleasure of observing a woman strip naked
on the opposite bank and then swim around in front of me. On another
occasion I admired two topless ladies drift past in a canoe one early
summer's morning and, twice now, I have had a kingfisher land on my
fishing rod whilst I was holding it. But the most remarkable thing I have
seen was a fisherman.

On the day I saw this individual there was a fishing course being run on
this stretch of river I was fishing. Six people were being guided by John
Bailey who just happens to be a man I have a great deal of respect for.
I had met most of the enthusiastic fishermen in the hotel the evening
before where fishing tales escalated in proportion as the evening gained
pace, just as they are meant to.

I had been fishing alone for so long that I was stuck in my own little
ways and I was in need of some fresh ideas, an insight into how others

fished and a little bit of company for a change. John said that he would leave me alone to do my own thing on the grounds that he reckoned I knew the river already. This was a mistake. I didn't. That's why I was on the course.

In the morning we were shown promising areas on the river before breakfast. Some I already knew, the others certainly got me thinking about how the hell I had missed them. When we got down to the actual fishing most people plonked themselves down in the places they fancied rather than the ones their guide had shown them. Rods were assembled, seats adjusted and baits started to hit the water at a frightening volume. It looked a bit of a static approach to me and there was an air of competition creeping in so I crept off and fished a few of the new areas I had just been shown.

It was deceptively warm for the time of year but the river was clear, cold and running low. With all that artillery hitting the water along with the increased activity on the bank I had this nagging suspicion that the fishing was going to be hard.

By mid-morning I was proved right, I hadn't caught a thing. So, as you do, I went for a stroll along the river to get some inspiration and to see how the others were getting on. They hadn't caught anything either (which made me feel a little less inadequate). We all chatted as we did a bit of head scratching. After a while there was nothing to do apart from get back in the river and try to catch a fish. Walking along the river's edge I saw this figure stood in the water fishing differently to everybody else. Instead of sitting behind motionless fishing rods he was fishing a run of water with a float and centrepin reel. He was fishing it good too.

Having caught some barbel from this little glide before I knew it could be a good place, especially when the weather was bright like this. The overhanging trees offered some of the only shade on the river and fish aren't too keen on bright light, particularly in low water conditions.

It can get a bit uncomfortable for them with all that light bouncing about. Fish don't have eyelids and I've yet to see one sporting an expensive pair of sunglasses (even though I've dropped a few pairs in the river myself) so they tend to avoid it unless they feel like sunbathing or the sun has attracted other creatures that the fish can eat.

I knew from the chat the evening before that the man I was looking at had never fished this stretch of the Wye but, there was no doubt about it, he had made a good choice. Normally I would give another angler a wide berth on the reasoning that they may enjoy their solitude as much as I do, but I was intrigued by the way he approached the river. I knew I wasn't going to catch anything so I thought I would watch somebody who looked as though they might.

Crouching below the skyline, like a good boy, I put my rod down on the grass and kept as quiet as I could and watched. There was no hurry with what he was doing. His float ran down the river beautifully. He controlled that float so that it skirted the crease in the water which is exactly where any hungry fish was likely to be. He fished in a very casual manner but beneath the peak of his cap you could see the gaze of a fine fisherman. He fished instinctively yet his attention to detail was precise. His float was handmade, had a large tip so that it could be seen at distance and a fluted elder pith body that gripped the water rather than sliding with it. The whole set up was balanced so that the float could be held back allowing the bait (tripping over the bed of the river) to travel at the same speed as the free offerings of food that he was introducing by hand in a steady imitation of Nature herself. This was thoughtful fishing. This was good fishing. Very good fishing indeed. It was a long time since I had seen such intensity of concentration combined with obvious pleasure. He was fishing a float a lot better than I will ever be able to, so I regarded it as a piece of education that needed to be absorbed - something my school teacher believed I was incapable of. I was surprised that his float didn't bury itself immediately as a monster barbel fell for the beautifully presented bait. It really was a remarkable sight. I was quite in awe of the skill he transmitted through the rod and down the line to the float. The way he used that rod was graceful, like watching a skilled fly-fisherman delicately drop his imitation so that it rested on the surface film like a piece of thistledown, except he was doing it with a fifteen foot float rod. It was very impressive.

He knew I was watching but he continued as if mesmerized by the river, welded to it though a length of fishing line. After a little while he stopped and joined me on the bank where we talked of fishing and of rivers in particular. He talked of his love for the Hampshire Avon, of long trotting for roach and how he got to designing the floats he was using. I talked of the Wye, her occupants and the grip she held on me since the first time I saw her and of how I had found her frighteningly powerful before familiarity turned her in to a lover. He seemed to approve of my old split cane rod and there was a chemistry which simply developed over a shared passion.

We were in danger of doing more talking than fishing so I picked out a big worm from a bag and asked, 'Have you tried a lobworm?' He hadn't, so I lent him one. It seemed the right thing to do.

He waded out into the water to give himself a straight line to work his magic, threaded the worm onto the hook, adjusted the float to counteract the slightly heavier bait, peeled the line from the reel, flicked out the tackle and eased the bait towards the trees. As it entered the shade he held it back a little. I imagined the worm rising slightly, a very tempting sight for a hungry fish. He had a fish first cast. It was his first barbel from the river Wye.

I have come across a great deal of people on the banks of rivers, ponds, lakes and reservoirs and after many years of watching I can tell you this - I've seen a man fishing badly but I've yet to see a bad man fishing. This individual was neither. He ranks right up there with the very best. A combination of competence, attention to detail and pure undiluted enjoyment sets him apart.

Even so, friendship is an entirely different thing altogether and that takes time. An understanding develops through familiarity into an almost telepathic state. Moods are judged, ambitions shared and you both instinctively know when it is time to break down the rods, call it a day and make plans for the next meeting. And that, is exactly what we did after we released that young barbel.

I have been fishing with Phil Humm on a regular basis ever since we met on that bright October day and that is many years back now. I have had a lot of fun along the way but I still haven't got that worm back!

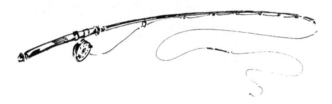

PARADISE

BARBEL - THE RIVER WYE

The real challenge with fishing is to find somewhere
where nobody else goes.

Paradise, in fishing terms, is a place where the river flows clear, with pools and glides and gurgling eddies. Where the weed sways to the rhythm of the current, where fish are obliging, the butterflies play with the mayflies as a kingfisher watches and the swallows conduct the orchestra from above. It is a place where nobody else goes, a place where you can lie in the grass, close your eyes and soak it all in forgetting about everything else, a place that leaves you with the very pleasing thought that this is what you are meant to be doing - sitting about with a fishing rod by your side and water in front of you. As you can imagine, finding paradise isn't easy. To find it requires planning, a certain amount of leg work and a large dollop of imagination. It took us a while, but we got there in the end.

After a great deal of talking and a little bit of that planning Phil and myself pushed our way through the undergrowth, lacerating our arms and getting stung on our faces by the nettles as we edged ourselves towards a very inaccessible part of the river just to have a look at the potential and to get away from the other fishermen. Once we got there we realised why no one comes down here. It didn't look that good.

Unlike most of the river it appeared uniform, slow running and (especially when raining) grey. The best we could say were deep and meaningful things like, 'Well it might be alright.' And, 'There has got to be fish around here – hasn't there?' But one thing was certain, if we were looking for solitude this was the place and that was good enough for me.

The end result of all that poking about was that on the first day of the following season we scraped our way back through the jungle with fishing rods, cameras and anything else that could get caught up in the trees. The vegetation was denser and sharper than I remembered. These were the days before we had discovered Gortex, and the warm day was emphasized by wearing rubber chest waders. It wasn't easy, but when we got there the sun bounced through the trees and gave the river a new perspective turning the previous sepia image into one of a brightly lit Renaissance painting. The sort of thing that has you looking deeper and deeper and finding a lot more than you expected as a result.

Now that the river level had dropped the push of water looked more attractive. A crease in the water created a 'V' that pointed to some rapids downstream. Mid-river a huge forest of ranunculus weed had reappeared though spring which made me realise that there are things under water that make a freshly moan lawn look dull. The white of the flowers acted as jewellery and the trees on both sides had sprouted their leaves that formed a tunnel down the river that concentrated the illusion of a wilderness. From the top of the high bank it was like looking into a dream – clear water, clean gravel and lush vegetation that swayed to the rhythm in a beautiful, flaunty and very sexy dance. We saw no fish.

Loosening the waders to let some air in (and the condensation out) we collapsed and gazed towards the heavens. We watched a pair of buzzards watching us watching them and our minds floated away as a blanket of silence comforted us. If there was any doubt as to whether or not this was paradise, the fact was circled with a golden highlighter pen as I glimpsed an angel from the corner of my eye.

'Barbel'

'Where?'

'Right in amongst the weed.'

'Sure?'

'Sure.'

'I see her.'

One fish turned into two, then three, four, five until there were about twenty fish treating us to an aquatic firework display as they twisted and flashed and illuminated the river with their sparks.

Moments like this heave you up to heaven and spiral you towards the spiritual plain that cradles this valley whilst at the same time they glide you back down to earth and make you realise that the effort of putting in the effort was worth it. The whole experience circled around as quietly as those buzzards above and as purposefully as the fish below. We were simply caught up in the middle of things.

It is not often that you come across such a congregation of fish so we kept looking, looking at each other and then looking back at the fish. It took a while before it dawned upon us that we could actually fish for what we were looking at. It was at this stage that I made my way down the steep bank as Phil directed me to the *exact* spot we had agreed would be a good place to put some bait out to try and get the fish feeding.

Expectation hung heavy over the river like an early morning mist as I inched my way across slippery rocks and onto the gravel getting closer to the fish. One thing was for sure, no matter how much I tried to kid myself, they knew I was there. They always do.

Above the chuckle of running water I could hear a grasshopper in the opposite field and at the same time there were wild fish gliding in and out of the weed within spitting distance. When the opportunity is as good as this one, your legs wobble and you become very aware of any noise you're making. I was doing alright - just.

Then, down the funnel of trees, came a sound so out of place that it made me cringe. I shut my eyes and cursed. Phil was still urging me on but he couldn't see what I could. Then it swung into his view.

A fifteen foot aluminium canoe slashed it's way towards me before veering towards the far bank. The jolly mariners dragged it up the shingle and got out to have a leak. With the surface tension of the water acting like a drum and the high banks acting as an amplifier it sounded like the opening chord of a Led Zeppelin concert.

It took them longer than I thought was necessary but when the three pioneers finished farting they paddled back to wherever they had come from, Davey Crocket style.

The fish had gone but I put the bait in anyway and rejoined my partner to sit down, hold our heads in our hands and pray. It seemed an appropriate moment to be converted to some ancient faith.

The whole episode had taken a few minutes. It seemed a lot longer. It also seemed one long way to paddle just to relieve yourself, but then I suspect they thought I was a little odd standing in the middle of an otherwise uninhabited stretch of river holding a couple of cans of sweet corn whilst wearing a silly hat and a pair of expensive shades.

In paradise there is meant to be a God. I have never been a great believer myself yet, as those barbel materialised once again, I began to understand why this faith thing has lasted thousands of years and realised that there may just be something in it. Things then got crazy. Where there had been twenty fish before there were now upwards of thirty. We tried to take our time but excitement took over. So we went fishing.

We were careful, quiet and fished intelligently. We didn't get a touch. I thought I had, but looking back I think that was just my way of lessening the fact that we were stood in the middle of a shoal of fish with straight fishing rods. After a long time of convincing ourselves that we were going to latch into a three foot long barbel we sloshed ashore. Frustration had crept in, yet, with the buzzards still watching, the sun enhancing the river and a mink scuttling along the bank behind us, I realised that this was as close to heaven as I was likely to get. I sat and absorbed it whilst discussing with Phil how we could make contact with one of those fish. After a bit of thought we did the only thing we could think of. We went for breakfast.

We were staying at the local vicarage where our breakfast table was all set out by a window that overlooks a garden that cascades down to the river. We have been staying here on short fishing trips long enough for our hosts to know that one of us doesn't like tomatoes and the other one always leaves the white of the egg. That one of us drinks lots of coffee, the other lots of tea, that we get up at ridiculously uncivilised times of the morning and don't vacate the local bar until it's shut and even then we need some reminding. The really nice thing about it all is that nobody seems to mind, and they instinctively know whether that particular morning is a good time to ask us if we have caught any fish. They didn't ask this morning. By the way, thanks very much Charles and Wendy for the hospitality.

    We fished elsewhere for the remainder of the day and in the evening retired to the hotel bar which was full of other people trying to work out why they hadn't caught anything either. They were all looking at one man who was expected to put them onto some fish.

    John Bailey was bearing up quite well considering the lack of fish. John guides anglers on stretches of river like this one, helping people get the most out of it and, hopefully, getting them a fish or two in the process. Some choose to ignore his advice but I suppose at the end of the day they are paying for the privilege. Personally, if he suggested I try float fishing a freshly killed minnow underneath that clump of trees on the near bank first thing in the morning I would try not to stay up too late and get up real early in case somebody had overheard the conversation.

    Phil and myself have got to know John well over the years and we have become good friends in the process. We told him about the barbel and he asked to have a look after he had finished his guiding the next day.

    In the morning Phil and myself revisited paradise as if something profound was about to happen. The barbel were still there and we were getting used to the tricks the current played with the tackle. It would simply be a matter of casually rolling a big, juicy, natural worm down to the fish and waiting for the inevitable arm wrenching battle. We fished for about three hours without a bite before giving up and trying elsewhere.

At five o'clock precisely, we met John by the church and then all trudged back to paradise. Initially it looked as though the fish had gone, but then they showed as if someone had flicked a light on. There were some attempts at trying to get some photographs. A lot of, 'Nice fish moving in,' and, 'How many do you reckon there are?' After over an hour of admiration I tossed in several handfuls of corn and we left them alone.

I was going to return in the morning so I was content. John was going back to see how his course members were getting on, so he was apprehensive and Phil was being forced to pack up his belongings, stuff them into his car and make the very long journey home so that he could go to work. I find it hard to remember ever having seen a more depressed individual.

It felt strange cutting my way down there the next day without my fishing partner, as though I was trespassing. When I got there I sat on a little stump, high up on the edge of the bank and tried to slow myself down to match the pace of the surroundings. 'This time,' I said, 'we'll have one.'

As I slipped down into the little clearing there was just me, the river and the fish. I released the hook from the cork handle on the rod, slipped two grains of sweet corn on as bait and made the cast.

I caught two fish. Neither were dream sized, but they were beautiful. I got my photograph as I laid the first fish on the soft weed and when I released her I realised how wild a creature it was that I had just let go. She hung in the push of water and nosed around the gravel bed of the river by my feet, as if nothing had happened. She then eased around and sailed across to her relatives like a seagull wheeling the wind. She reclaimed her position in the group and, having followed her all the way, it was clear to see that there were some very long fish out there. I made another cast and caught the second fish. I then left them alone. It seemed the right thing to do.

Finding paradise had absolutely nothing to do with luck. Hooking that first fish did. I just reeled in for a recast, felt a tug and there she was. That's not something I would generally admit to freely but on this occasion I didn't so much catch that fish. I was given it.

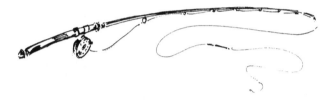

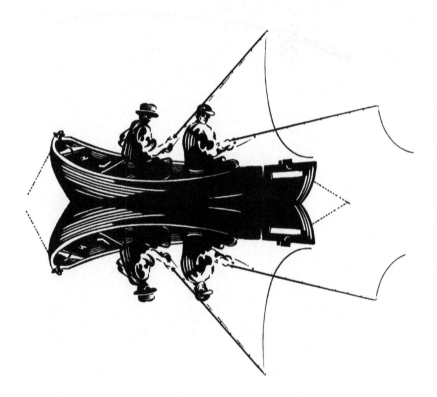

ENTOMOLOGY

TROUT - ESSEX

You don't realise how much you need to go fishing
until somebody tells you that you can't.

The foot and mouth virus was devastating our countryside. Six million
animals had been slaughtered and there was more to come. Farmyards fell
silent as the skies filled with the black acrid smoke of the 'funeral' pyres
signalling that this was not a good place to be. Walking in the countryside
became impossible because of the restrictions. Television showed us the
killing fields on an hourly basis and we all became familiar with a deadly
virus that liked the cold weather, spread like a forest fire, moved in the air
currents and, like the rest of us, didn't understand politics. The farmers
were suffering, so was the tourist industry. The government delayed the
National Election and then announced that the countryside was open
again. The guardians of every stretch of river I knew continued to tell
me it was closed. It was a great tragedy. Fishing was out of the question,
and it was beginning to attack a basic instinct I have, to the extent that I
could be seen hanging around the fishmonger's stall in the market square
on Friday lunchtimes in the hope of being able to rub some fish slime
onto my jeans. I needed a fix. I needed one real bad. So I rang my dealer.

Phil, my dealer, checked out his contacts and came up with a solution
at a frightening speed. It wasn't exactly crack cocaine he was offering but
it was a healthy alternative. He had found somewhere to fish.

Arriving at Phil's house, the evening before the arranged trip, it
became obvious that I wasn't the only person who was getting cabin

fever. Mick Bay and Simon MacMillan, (both of whom I have fished with in the past) were already drinking cold beer and browsing through some photographs of Mick's recent trip to India. We all marvelled at the beauty of the mahseer he'd caught and then went to the pub where we talked a little more about fishing.

Early in the morning we drove to the fishery, set up five weight fly rods and handed over what I considered rather more money than was necessary for a four fish limit and a couple of boats. As you'd expect in a crisis, there were a lot of other people there so it wasn't a good time to negotiate the price.

To begin with we didn't have much luck. None of us are what you could call 'fly-fishers'. We weren't exactly up to scratch on the entomology stakes and we couldn't identify all those complicated sounding names given to flies like, Green Drake Mayfly, Viva Marabou, Black Spectral Spider or Bubble Sedge Hare's Ear that we heard being enthusiastically talked about in the fishing hut. Most of the other fishermen looked the part with all the fly-fishing clothing, implements and, presumably the knowledge. They were casually drinking tea and talking about these things in a dead language called Latin. But, 'Hey', we've caught fish before, it can't be that difficult to catch them on a fly. All we needed to do was study the water intently, scrutinise any visible fly life, match the size of the hook to the size of whatever we saw. Then, open up the fly box and select the required 'what ever it was' and go fishing.

Phil went for the fluffy white thingy and I went for the fluffy green one. Our expertise paid off in less than an hour as Phil tapped into a fish and I, quite understandably, changed my fluffy green thingy for a fluffy white one. The light values and barometric pressure had changed slightly since I made my original selection - it was an intellectual decision to make the change, you'll understand?

Once we had determined what depth the trout we're feeding at and what sort of retrieve to use, we had them lunging at the lures and the fishing became easy.

All the fish were around the two to three pound mark - good fighters too - nice to look at - real tasty when lightly grilled with a squeeze of lemon and a twist of black pepper. We were doing all right.

I put out another clumsy cast, much the same as all the others, started a slow, jerky retrieve and then felt a bang on the end of the line. The little white fluffy thing had done it again. This time the fish didn't leap out of the water or streak away like the others had done. It hung low and steady with a pace that indicated something of substance.

At first I thought I had hooked a pike. Then I saw the unmistakable flash of a rainbow trout. It was one of those moments that has you looking at your fishing partner to check whether he had seen it too. He had, he was picking up the net as if to say, 'You'd better not lose this one, Rob.' But, like good fishing partners do, he didn't say a word.

It took a while to get that fish up to the surface. Once it saw us, it started fighting like trout are meant to and I started getting worried about the three pound breaking strain tippet I was using. At one stage, it made a go for the anchor rope (which would have been the end of the fun) but Phil managed to get the inadequately sized net under her. The head of the fish stuck out over the net at one side and the tail did the same at the other. This thing looked like Bob Dylan's mattress balancing on a bottle of wine. Once the juggling act was over we dragged her into the boat like Ernest Hemmingway wrestling with a marlin. Once on board, we peeled back the netting and just started laughing. This was one big trout. What had looked big in the water now looked ridiculous, I mean, trout just aren't meant to grow that big. I'll admit she looked impressive, but she wasn't what I would call a real fish. The profile of her head was wrong, the thickness of her tail odd, the markings on her flank were so far apart that they didn't work together, her eye seemed small and her adipose fin was the size of a bad blacksmith's thumb. Man had reared a trout of such ridiculous proportions that it was sad.

The fishing permit stated that all fish caught had to be killed. This presented us with a bit of a problem. Because we have never got around to buying one of those posh priests made from brass and antler from a Highland stag (as seen in the fly-fishing catalogues) the smaller fish had been dispatched with a sharp tap on the back of the head with the handle of my knife, but this mother wasn't going to be frightened by a tiny little tickle like that. We looked around to make sure nobody could see us before locating a more suitably sized implement – we used the anchor! It was only after the echo of the thud had subsided and the ripples had tired themselves out that we realised that we could have put a hole in the boat and got ourselves very wet.

That fish was far from a world record or anything like that, but the size of it was crazy compared to the trout I was used to catching. It had also taken us up to the four fish limit on the ticket. So, rods were put down, the oars taken up and we returned to shore to stretch the old sea legs and do a little bragging.

Although we had reached our limit, we had paid for the boats for the rest of the day. A couple of other friends had arrived to join us because the foot and mouth had affected their fishing too and word on the street had got around as to where we were. We didn't want to sit it out on dry land watching somebody else having all the fun, so we paid a bit more money (actually it was quite a lot more money) allowing us to fish the afternoon through – as long, we were emphatically told, as any fish we caught were put back. This was fine by me. Hell, one of us was already going to have to gut and clean twenty four trout, because our friends were guaranteed to catch their limit, just as long as they knew their entomology and used the little white fluffy thingy as the rest of us had been doing.

After the financial transactions had been dealt with, the ticket salesman watched us get back into the boats and it didn't take too long for us to get back into the fish. There were now six fluffy white thingys being cast towards the obliging trout. For most of the afternoon it seemed as though at least one rod was bent into a fish. It was good fun out there.

I haven't a clue how many fish we caught and released but it was lots. The little white fluffy thing hanging from the end of my line was looking a bit battered. In an attempt to prove my superior knowledge of the local aquatic insect life and my acute observation that the light values had changed once again, I changed the white fluffy thingy for a pristine orange fluffy one. It didn't work so I shrugged my shoulders and stated that I only tried the orange one to get a greater understanding of the situation. I then put the shredded white pattern back on and I started to catch fish again.

It doesn't always happen like this and, usually, if it does, something goes horribly wrong. Today's tragedy materialised in the form of the fishery owner. Everybody else had packed up and gone home. We were the only ones left. With such tremendous sport, I couldn't understand why everybody else hadn't paid the extra for a catch and release ticket once they had reached their limit but, I suppose, that was their choice.

Sat out in the boats it was a little difficult to work out what the fishery owner was trying to yell at us. So we did the polite thing. We all pulled up the anchors and headed ashore in unison like the Spanish Armada. As we got closer you could see he didn't look too happy. When we got within hearing range (and this man could shout) he cupped his hands around his mouth and bellowed, 'You boys do know that this isn't the catch and release lake, don't you?'

We all looked at each other and made innocent looking gestures, like a premiership football player who has just been given the yellow card for a lunging foul. And, why not? We were innocent. I've fished on plenty of waters where I couldn't make that claim but we had paid for a catch and release ticket, the ticket salesman had watched us paddle back out, all the additional fish we caught had been slipped off the barbless hooks and released immediately. We had done everything we had been asked to do. So who was to blame here?

When we got ashore, the fishery owner mellowed. Maybe it was because there were six of us and one of him and the fact that our explanation of events was entirely plausible. Anyway, he accepted the mistake and asked us how many of his trout we had hooked. The figure was put to him in the kindest possible way when someone replied, 'Quite a few.' To be fair, this chap was quite apologetic about the situation. He even said we could fish on if we wanted to, but we declined that one because we all knew that we had hooked well over a hundred of his trout, so we broke down the rods and cleaned out the boats.

Before we left, it was decided to have a little competition to see who could guess the weight of the big trout before we put it on the scales outside the fishery hut. The only thing I could equate this fish to was a barbel and I wasn't far off with a guess of eleven pounds four ounces. As it turned out, Dave Wilson, one of the late arrivals, got it bang on the nose with an estimate of eleven fourteen and gained himself a free King Prawn Biryani with Mushroom Rice in the process.

I spent the change from the Indian meal on some size 12 Gold Head Catswhiskers, with a twist of silver thread running along the shank, that had been tied onto a wide gape, barbless, chemically sharpened hook. That's a white fluffy thing, in case you were wondering.

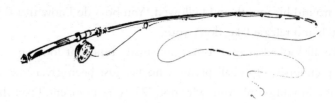

CUTTING IT DOWN

OTHER FISHERMEN - THE RIVER WYE

Sometimes I spend so much time fishing on my own
that I begin to wonder what I am doing wrong.

I heard him well before I saw him. There was this sort of clanking noise coming up the river that had me poking my head above the foliage to see what was going on. The sun was in my eyes but I could make out the silhouette of another fisherman struggling along the high banks of the river. I watched him for a while and then he spotted me. I must have startled him because he dropped down into the professional fisherman's stoop (keep low on the skyline, find the fish, look as though you know what you're doing, all those sorts of things). He then straightened up, adjusted his luggage and started walking again.

It was fairly obvious he was trying to find a place to pin his hopes on for the day, but he was indecisive and getting dangerously close to where I was. It was time to take a deep breath, clear the throat loudly and adopt a casual male pose that radiates, 'Hey, I don't mind other fishermen but you're getting mighty close – Mister!'

It didn't work. He kept on coming, so I hoisted myself up onto the bank, rested my back against a tree, absorbed the sunshine and waited for the inevitable meeting. It was pointless moving. He was hard to focus on because the sun was in my eyes, but I could tell he had the determination of a bull and he was closing in.

Then I got to thinking, why should he be a he? After all, there are plenty of female fishers out there, and, before you ask yourself the question – the ones I've met are pretty good at it too. Sure, you don't see too many unaccompanied (which in today's society is something I can fully understand) but the thought did make me drop my guard. Thoughts of, 'This bastard is going to drop in next to me,' were replaced by 'What is it?' It was all getting a bit unnerving so I collected my rod and small bag, tossed them up the bank and returned to the comfort of the tree trunk – let's face it, the approaching silhouette knew where I was fishing but it didn't need to know *exactly* where.

The vision was now so close I heard it break wind and at that stage, I knew it was a male of the species. Women anglers do a lot of things us fellows do, but that isn't generally one of them.

As he entered the shade of the tree, he expelled a wheezing sound from his lungs that went, 'Jeeesh!' He then wiped his brow with his baseball cap and dropped a landing net, rod rest, stainless steel thermos flask, bait bucket, collapsible chair, three hundred pounds worth of carbon fibre, a fourteen foot long keepnet, bag of groundbait, set of scales, a four pack of John Smith's Best Bitter, a set of expensive waterproofs and a very large umbrella. The last two items had me looking around for storm clouds. There weren't any. But at least I now knew where that clanking sound had come from.

He was the first to break into conversation.

'Fancy a beer?'

'Cheers.'

'Nice morning, hey?'

'Was earlier.'

I cracked open the can and glanced at my watch. It told me it was time to go home, but I stayed. This was going to be interesting. He had every bit of tackle I had ever seen in the mail order catalogues. Please don't get me wrong, he was a nice enough chap (he had just given me a beer) but, with that amount of kit, he was about to make a fool of himself or make me very annoyed, very quickly, by emptying the river of fish right in front of my eyes.

'Caught anything?' He asked.

'Not here.' I replied.

'Great place for chub this. Sure you ain't had any chub?'

I was sure.

I had been on the river for five hours. Fished it for about two. I related the truth, told him I had a couple of small barbel further downstream on float fished casters, told him I had seen a nice fish roll but hadn't been able to tempt her. He looked at me as a judge looks at the defendant and repeated;

'Really great place for chub, this.'

'Really.' I said.

He had won. I had just been bullied out of a place where I had been quite happy doing a little fishing of my own and watching a heron do hers. On the reasoning that he had just scared every fish within eight hundred yards by dropping all that kit, I sort of gave way.

Sensing that I was going to leave he started to set up his tackle with confidence and I was given a running commentary of exactly what he was doing, using, adapting, unscrewing and intending to achieve with the end result that I got mighty confused with all the complications.

There I was, in the great outdoors, watching the type of instructional lesson I didn't want or even felt was necessary. Still, it did make me realise that maybe, just maybe, there was more to fishing than I had realised. I have got to admit that this man had precision. Not only did he have all the gadgets, he actually used them. I could learn something here.

When I tie on a hook, I usually add a little saliva to the line to lubricate it and help it all slide neatly together as the knot is tightened. It's one of those little things that make sense and we all got taught as kids. This chap not only wet his line, he snipped off the loose ends with some expensive nail clippers even though he appeared to have a perfectly good set of teeth. He then secured the finished knot with super glue. Classy! He even sharpened the hook.

Occasionally I test the strength of the knot by looping the hook over the bail arm of the reel and giving it a steady tug. He had a special knot tightener. It equated to the same thing, except his cost money, was designed for the specific purpose, had a logo emblazoned upon it and was another gadget. The line he was using looked dangerously thin to me - but who was I to say? There was no doubt about it, this was organisation on a scale I didn't realise existed. Everything was pristine. The rod looked like it had just come out of the wrapper. The reel gleamed in the sunlight. Beneath his jacket he wore a waistcoat from which hung all the surgical necessities - forceps, scissors, disgorgers, thermometer - all attached to retractable little clips. Nothing was out of place. He was obviously a firm favourite at the local tackle shop.

His thigh waders looked new and were rolled down to knee height in a fashion that not only looks damned stupid but also renders the purpose of the garment totally useless. Under his waistcoat hung a plastic apron with more pockets, into one of which he poured a generous helping of maggots. He wore a woollen top underneath that and he was looking very warm.

I was obviously under dressed for the occasion wearing some dungarees from West Midland Farmers discount store, a pair of five year old leather boots (from Farlows, Pall Mall, if you don't mind) a T-shirt from a recent Neil Young tour and a wide brimmed hat with a quill float stuck in the band. I felt a little like a hillbilly in comparison, but I was nice and cool (heat wise, not in the fashion sense, you'll understand).

This man's patience was amazing. Instead of fishing, he unleashed a second rod and started to repeat the process. Warm beer under the even warmer sun can make you a little sarcastic, so I asked, 'What time do you plan to fish?'

'Got a couple of fellow club members coming down at twelve for a friendly competition,' he replied.

The words 'friendly' and 'competition' have never seemed to slot together too well so I made my excuse and left my tutor with the customary 'Good luck,' and an empty can.

Sauntering back along the river, I approached a small over hanging willow where I could almost guarantee at least one good chub if I wasn't being watched. There were two other fishermen pegged in for the day a little downstream and I was being watched.

Nobody really cared what I was doing, but I did feel guilty when I whipped on a size 4 forged (this ain't going to bend for nobody) hook, and threaded on three chunks of luncheon meat that emptied half a can and left a hefty bend in the rod. There was no need for any additional weight because the current here rolls a freelined bait beautifully underneath the bush, so I chewed off the link of nylon that attached it and waded out to have that one cast.

You only ever get one chance here, get it wrong and you frighten the fish and that chance has gone – it is as simple as that. Miss that chance and you may as well pack up and walk away because it isn't going to happen. No matter how many fish you can still see, and what ever approach you think of, you are not going to catch. Believe me, I have wasted a lot of time stood in the middle of that bit of river. I once crept out there without a fishing rod to have a real good look. The water was three feet deep and running clear. I was with a fishing friend named John Ferebee at the time. He poked his head through the low slung branches only to reappear with his hair dripping wet, pronouncing, 'Jesus, I could live in there.'

As he said that, the rightful occupants bolted downstream, over rocks, sunken branches and between my legs. It was quite a sight. The chub came first followed by the barbel, although you would have needed a good stop–watch and an action replay to gauge the exact time difference.

The order in which they came out shocked me a little but there was no doubting what I had seen. This place had always looked an ideal chub swim but the presence of the barbel surprised me and I realised that you shouldn't believe everything you read in books about barbel, gravel and fast currents. Now, every time I pass the place, I wonder whether today's the day that the chub will leave the bait alone long enough for that barbel to get a look in. When I say *that* barbel, it should be obvious that *that* means it is one hell of a good fish. 'Size doesn't matter,' is a phrase used by fishermen that really means, 'Well, it does sometimes.'

If you don't spook the chub, they will take a cigarette butt flicked onto the surface but as soon as you hook one, it panics the rest. So you tend to approach the place with the mentality of, 'Can I walk across twenty yards of rice paper wearing studded wading boots without creasing it?' If you can, you wade back after releasing the fish with the casual self-satisfaction of the football player who scored the deciding goal in the European Cup penalty shoot out. You would prefer to label this as clever but you know that really it was easy. All the same, you remember that it's only possible if you know where the spot is in the first place.

So there I was, half way across the river, with those two other fishermen trying to work out what I was doing, wading slowly, thinking 'Right Rob, show these boys how to whip out a fish,' then I thought, 'What am I doing?' For three years I had only fished this little patch of shade when alone or with what I would describe as a solid friend. I don't even fish it that often because I haven't figured out a way of selecting that barbel and I wouldn't prove anything by hammering it. The fish would simply move out and I would have to move on. Neither would be very happy about that. Fish it. Respect it. Then leave it alone - sounds about right to me, so I stopped and glanced at the fishermen to my right. The large bait swung in mid-air, ticking out the pendulum of indecision, whilst I tried to figure out whether to continue or retreat.

I thought it out, thought of the future and retreated. It was a shame for the place looked just right. The sun was off the water, the current gave the surface that calm, glazed look and the fish would definitely be there. All the same, I had to ask myself whether the secrecy of the place was more important than what it held. I broke the rod down, adjusted the hat, strolled back through the water and walked back to the car to make the journey home, telling myself I had just done something worthwhile. I had.

When I get back from a fishing trip, I generally play football with my boy, get something to eat, take off the boots, have a wash and collapse. Not necessarily in that order. Although I occasionally think about it, cleaning out the back of the car always waits until next week and there is no point doing it then because you are going fishing again.

It makes little difference to me whether I've been out for a few days or just the usual morning - I always feel the same - tired. Whoever it was who said that fishing was the height of relaxation was either a natural liar or didn't fish the way most of the people I know do.

Usually I forget about the fishing once I am home, but on this day I couldn't stop wondering how that chap had got on in the 'friendly competition.' Had I got it all wrong? Had I trimmed my own tackle down to such an extent that I didn't have any left? Did I need to go out and spend some money? Was this why I hadn't caught many fish recently?

Helen had taken the opportunity of my return to stroll into town. Tom was upstairs having an afternoon nap (which is something only young boys and old men are allowed to do). I dragged out my tackle bag from the back of the car, sat on the front door step with a cup of tea and started to sort out what I had. It wasn't much.

I had been using a small camera bag to carry my tackle. In one of the front pockets there was a selection of hooks, size 4 through to size 14. In the other was the usual collection of leads - round ones, flat ones, bullet shaped ones, all of them were pretty light. There was also a small packet of little plastic plugs that I sometimes use to stop these leads sliding too far down the line and there was a coil of old line that I removed and stuffed into my jacket pocket where it probably still remains.

Inside the bag was my camera, a second lens, and a flash gun that I haven't quite learned to use properly. There was also a little box that contains hooks with cunning little pieces of cork glued on, in an attempt (and I do mean attempt) to make the hooks appear weightless once in the water. They're shaped and painted to resemble the baits I add to the hook - sweet corn, casters, maggots, hemp. I don't use them that often, but they do look very pretty and they took me a long time to make so I'd feel fairly naked without them. Another little box contains the only other sundries you are likely to need - a few swivels, beads and float rubbers.

At the back of the bag were some spare spools of line and a tube containing a few floats and two lengths of peacock quill. I had a look at these and decided that some of them I would never use on the river, so instead of adding tackle, I started taking it out.

There was also a small set of lovely old brass pocket scales and a roll of unprocessed 50 ASA Fuji transparency film. That was it. I took the scales out because I'd stopped using those, too.

If you forget the camera, the whole lot weighs less than the can of beer the chap had given me. It didn't look like much when it was spread out on the front door steps, so I began to wonder what I was missing.

I dug out the rod and landing net and realised that, apart from the bait, I didn't have anything left. Sure, I own an umbrella, but it's under a load of other junk in the garage - I think! I don't like umbrellas for the same reason I leave the rod rests at home - they pin you down. These days, when it rains I pull the hat down tight and lift the collar up, get wet and carry on fishing.

I wasn't missing anything. In fact I had just spent a good eight years cutting it down to the level it was at now and I am pretty proud of that.

The only reason for adding things was so that I could announce my arrival by clanking up the river and that's the last thing I want to do.

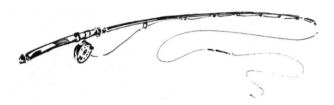

THE CIRCUS HAS GONE

*There is no greater feeling than arriving at a river
and finding that you are the only person there.*

The farm gate made a piercing groan. The cows in the shed stopped
eating and the dog appeared on the top of the wall, just as she always
does. She cocked her head, raised her right ear and gave me a show of
teeth just to let me know whose territory I was on. From the depths
of the cattle shed warm breath bellowed like a steam engine and its
occupants kept their eyes on me as I walked through the yard while the
dog followed my progress using the height of the wall to emphasise her
superiority. The studs on my boots made an embarrassing crunch that
sliced through the dawn. I glanced to my right to check that I hadn't
disturbed anybody in the farm house. There was a heron, statuesque, by
the little pond. She made eye contact and disappeared into the mist with
the silent flap of a poacher. The lights in the house were off. Farmers get
up early, fishermen get up earlier.

The noise from my steps softened as I hit the little mud track but the
dog was still with me, keeping her distance, staying low, catching up in
little bursts, skirting the puddles, using the raised ground between tractor
ruts as a highway. A real professional.

She stopped her vigil when I cranked open the final gate that led to
the river. I was still on her territory but she had decided I wasn't a real
threat. She had seen me often enough but always kept her distance. She
probably thought I was a bit weird. Let's face it, getting up at 4 o'clock

in the morning to try and catch a fish that you're going to let go must seem strange to a hungry dog. I sat on the top bar of the gate and gazed between a layer of green and the smoking water whilst the dog sniffed around the hedgerow. We were in no hurry. Overnight dew glistened like diamonds in the half-light. It was still, quiet and a little chilly. I scanned the field, looking for a bull that I had a close encounter with the previous weekend. He either wasn't there or was waiting in ambush. I stayed on the gate a little longer, it's best to be sure in situations like this.

I had been coming to this place most weekends during the summer to fulfil either an obsession, an instinct or through pure undiluted love, I am not sure which. The fishing hadn't been stunning in the number of fish caught but I had enjoyed it. It's a great place and I love the low water conditions with the clarity they bring. I adore the warmth of the sun on my skin, but I rarely catch many fish when the river's like this. Perhaps I get too absorbed in just being there. I don't know. Logic tells me that I should do really well. There are more hours in the day. You can watch those fish, work out an approach (it should be easier), but I rarely do as well in the summer months as I feel I should. This isn't a complaint. Fishing is a privilege. But on this day, as I sat on the gate, everything felt just fine. The seasons have changed, the landscape and temperature have smoothed, so has the river. There are no tyre tracks across the field, no footprints in the grass and the air smells fresh. I have the river to myself again. The circus has gone.

I assembled the rod whilst perched on the gate. The rod and tackle I had set up was nothing special. The bait I had planned to use was three great big lumps of luncheon meat. Hardly subtle, but that depends upon how you fish it. I had a plastic bag in my left hand pocket that contained two emptied cans of the stuff. Once I was happy with everything I started to walk and the dog followed, always keeping her distance. Half way across the field we both heard a tractor cough into life. Dennis was awake. The dog needed to go to work and I was left alone.

At a bend in the river (where an old hut lurches) I admired the body of water that was so full it hardly seemed to move. The water was high, coloured and running like mercury. She was back to a good healthy fighting weight. Not rising. Not falling. Autumn had arrived. Something urged me to take it easy and to approach the water with extreme caution. The fish would be nice and settled down but I would still need to approach the river as quietly as possible, no matter how cloudy the water the fish know you're there and the number one bait for catching a fish is caution.

After admiring the river for a few minutes I crushed the barb down on the hook and adjusted the hat. It was time to fish.

Walking upstream (well away from the water's edge) to the top of the beat I paused just before a boundary fence. I was looking at a steep bank with some overhanging trees. The trees had lost some of their appeal along with their leaves but the barbel would be close in, where the river runs deep and the current is as smooth as marble.

Several yards to my left there was a series of bushes and tangled tree roots that draped into the water diverting the current creating a comfortable pace of water. The barbel adore it.

Downstream, the water shallows as the current bulges over some formidable rocks. Even further down lies a sunken wall around which the fish can be seen feeding during the summer months and canoes get grounded. The place is reputed to be the haunt of monsters in the winter. I've never had one myself, but I can see why they would like it there but now, with the increase in velocity, the fish like this little patch of water in front of me. It was a good choice. Something was telling me that. I can't explain what, and I hope I never can.

I threaded the bait onto the hook and crept up so slowly that a pair of ducks caught the current and drifted across the river rather than panicking off like they usually do. It was a good sign.

The fish lay very close to a slight undercut in the bank. The bank itself is quite spongy near the edge and is capable of transmitting vibrations like a loudspeaker. It's not easy sliding down there without getting your head above the skyline so it takes some time. It's time worth taking. I made a judgement as to how much weight I needed to add to the line to hold bottom, crouched down on my haunches and lowered the bait into the current. I followed its path with the rod tip until it settled two feet from the bank. I was expecting an immediate response. I didn't get one.

Five minutes later I nudged the bait down a yard and concentrated on what was happening down there. I started to get tiny little plucks on the line that I could only just feel with my index finger. Strange, finicky, regular, little vibrations, like feeling your pulse. Not the usual fizz up the line you get when a barbel is deciding whether or not the bait is safe to take. Probably minnows attacking the large bait. Then I realised that it was a little late in the year for minnows to be a problem so the next time I felt the slightest pressure I hit into it. This was no minnow.

The fish shot into the main current and forged towards the rocks using the depth to her advantage. I could feel the contours of the river bed as she peeled over them like a low flying fighter plane doing a little bit of practice over the Black Mountains. There came a point where I couldn't let her go any further, a point where I had to cup my hand over the spool, apply maximum pressure, trust the knot strength and let the rod do its job. A little praying helped too. The fish turned, headed back against the current and decided to make things difficult by going for the undercut beneath my feet. I got her shortly afterwards but for a long time it had felt like a losing battle. All that time we were welded together by the magic of a fishing line.

I am afraid that I don't always look that delicate when I am playing a powerful fish. I've seen people cringe when I've lent into a fish and then cover their eyes when I decide it's time to stop her in her tracks, but, please believe me, this is the safest way to do it. It will not lose you a fish. More importantly, that fish can be released after a short rest. It hasn't been wandering all over the place for the last half hour because the man who was holding the rod was too scared to put a bend in it. Fishing rods are meant to bend, that's what they're designed for.

That fish was around the eight and a half pound mark. She was nice and healthy, kind of chunky. Fish of this stamp tend to stick together but I decided to leave the place alone for a while. I tossed a few torn off pieces of meat upstream so that they would trundle down to where that fish had come from and then I picked up the rod and went walkabout.

What I was looking for was another piece of water that had the same characteristics as the one I had just fished, the same pace, same depth, same obstruction to the current and where there was some security for the fish in the form of sunken trees, depressions, rocks or decaying weed beds. Having fished this stretch of river fairly often over the years I knew that there were three similar places. Far too similar to ignore, no matter how far the hike.

To get to the first one I had to walk around a big bend, negotiate another gate, slide down a little drop and then creep up to where a big oak tree overhangs the water. From here it was possible to get a cast in that rolled the bait into a nice depression beside some rocks. The water had the same characteristics as the first place I had fished but just laid out differently. There weren't any bushes in the water upstream but a broken down gate deflected the current in a similar way, leaving a crease on the water as though somebody had drawn a pencil line along it. I had a barbel first cast.

The next place I visited was quite a walk so when I got there I caught my breath. The water looked like tinted glass with a necklace of bubbles sliding along the surface at walking speed. There was a big snag upstream in the form of a sunken tree and rocks and gullies close in and

I fished underneath a tree whilst trying to hold on to stop myself slipping down the steep bank. It took a while to work out exactly where to make that all important first cast but shortly after I made it I felt the smallest pluck and I pinned it.

That fish took some landing as the angle and height I was fishing from was what you could call 'dangerous'. In the end I had to pass the rod around the tree trunk and then land the fish a little downstream where I could actually get to her. It all sounds easier than it was.

The place that fish had come from looked promising and I was sure that there were other fish down there but I didn't try again because, well, I had nearly fallen in, and I hadn't been wearing a life jacket and I didn't fancy the idea of killing myself for a fish. Particularly when there was nobody else about to recount my heroic demise. I like barbel a great deal, but not that much.

I was into a good morning here, one of those occasions when you fish and think hard about what you're doing whilst the reality of the thing is that everything was dropping into place nice and smoothly.

If I hadn't struck at the tiny sensation I had felt when I hooked that first fish I would still have been there with a straight fishing rod and very little enthusiasm. Instead I was walking the river with supreme confidence and the feeling that if I couldn't find another promising piece of water then I could just walk straight across the surface and try from the other side.

Before moving on I had a little sit down and got to thinking about the similarities between the three places I had fished, of how those fish had all taken such a large bait so gently. I began to wonder how many fish I had missed in the past because I mistook what was really a very delicate bite for a leaf hitting the line or a minnow attacking the bait. I came to the realisation that it was a lot.

In the past I have always tended to hit small bites, but these were different, these were minute. You had to close your eyes to heighten concentration so that you could detect them at all.

Time was running out. I had promised to be back home at lunchtime, but it was difficult to stop when the fishing was so interesting so I kept walking until the river stopped me in my tracks as if to say 'Have a go down here.' It was an easy place to fish, relatively flat, hopeless in low water conditions but exciting with a high river. Sometimes they are there, sometimes they are not. For some reason (which I haven't worked out yet) it's better to fish this place with an upstream cast and let the bait roll down in a straight line until it drops into a depression about two yards in front of a bush to the right. I re-checked the hook point and re-tied the knot. The current wasn't as fast here so I removed a little weight and made a long cast upstream before nudging the bait back until it rested where it felt comfortable.

The result was a very small indication and another fish.

Four fish from four different places in four casts is about as good as it can get. When people up here say that the fishing can be fantastic this is what they must mean.

Time was rushing past me but I couldn't resist one final cast in the place I had caught the first fish from so I made the long walk back and went through the whole procedure of crawling up on it again before I lowered the bait into the depths. The response was immediate and the thread that connects fish to fisherman turned in to the straightest line the river had ever seen.

This fish fought differently from the others. This was a big fish that had no intention of being obliging. The rod had quite a job to do and when the fish showed on the surface I knew it was something special. Why I did it I am not sure, but I slackened the clutch on the reel a little which was something she took full advantage of. I got her in the end but there was a certain degree of luck with that result.

This was the best fish of the morning, the best fish I ever had from this river if you measure these things in terms of size. For once I weighed her. It was more out of curiosity than trying to build up an ego. I then returned her to the river and headed for home. It was a good walk across the field. I don't remember it at all.

As I reached the farm the yard was full of sheep and Dennis and his dog were trying to get them into one of the pens. Dennis was doing a bit of stick waving but the dog was doing the majority of the work. I sat on the gate and watched. I like gates.

After the demonstration of what a good dog can do I slid down and chatted to Dennis.

'How was the fishing?' He asked.

'Beautiful.' I replied.

We then talked of the weather and other unimportant things as farmers and fishermen do. Whilst I was there I took out a chunk of luncheon meat from my pocket and held it out for the dog. As I continued to talk to Dennis, she sneaked up and took it from the palm of my hand. She lifted it off so gently that, if it hadn't been for the hint of warm breath and a slight release of pressure, I wouldn't have even known it had gone. It was a similar sensation to the one that I had felt running through the fishing line that morning and which had resulted in a minnow turning into a rather large fish.

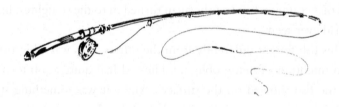

CONTACTING THE IMPOSSIBLE

SALMON - THE RIVER WYE

*If I were told that I could only catch one more fish before
I died I would say that it would have to be a salmon
from the Wye - that way I might live forever.*

It may have only been a whisper but the words sliced through the tranquillity of the hotel lounge as efficiently as if somebody had shouted, 'Oy. You over there!' To anybody else they may well have sounded quite innocent words but I took it all a bit personally. After all, there we were, being quiet, well behaved, spending money, when above the monotony of piped jazz music came a piercing description of myself and a very fine friend who was sat right next to me.

'The two in the corner? Just coarse fishermen.'

The hotel owner pointed from behind the security of the thick wooden bar as he spoke as his customer eyed us up and down with a degree of uncertainty that bordered on disgust. Having made his judgement he turned his back on us and ordered another gin and tonic.

'Did you hear that!?' I said.

'Yeah. What the hell does he mean by *just?*' Replied Phil.

I stared at the man who had glanced at me. There was nothing special about him except to say that he looked like the type of person who had access to more money than you can actually spend. Despite a fine set of tweeds, you could tell he was no farmer. I guessed he was a barrister. He had that air of authority that wreaks of arrogance and matched the very long, very thick, very expensive looking cigar that he had just ignited. I imagined him dismissing us with a 'Oh, don't worry, those boys couldn't catch a salmon if they tried.'

We were left with two choices. We could sneak out of the door and let the tyres down on the gleaming XJ6 Jaguar parked by the front of the hotel or we could finish our drinks, mumble a polite, 'Cheers old boy,' and catch ourselves a salmon. Seeing as how I gave up the thought of vandalising cars when I bought my own we went fishing with a hint of enthusiasm. Look at it this way, we may not have caught a salmon before but this wasn't the first time we had been salmon fishing.

When you visit this particular hotel on a fairly regular basis it's inevitable that you get to talking about fish, especially when you consider that nearly everybody who stays here owns at least one fishing rod. When the hotel in question has a great history of salmon fishing it figures that talk of this majestic fish is going to crop up regularly. In fact, it cropped up so often that we decided we'd actually give this salmon fishing a go. We were aware that the fish stocks were nothing like they used to be and that it wasn't going to be easy but we also knew that we had seen salmon in the river. And to hell with it, we're fishermen. When you pull one out every cast you stop and take up something less challenging – like cloning sheep.

As a result, several weeks earlier, myself, Phil and a couple of other fishermen that we had been introduced to decided that we would like to try for one of these things called a salmon. We suggested a weekend and Mike Taylor, the hotel owner, arranged it. It all seemed so simple – fine accommodation, breakfast in the mornings, beer in the evenings, four miles of river at our disposal, two days to fish them and gillie thrown in.

When the big day arrived there we were, being instructed in the rudiments of salmon fishing, by the local expert who had a wonderful name for a fisherman – Ron Rudd. Ron took us down to the river, convinced us that we were in with a chance of a fish (and that was a fine bit of convincing) and then handed me a fifteen foot double handed fly rod with a big reel attached and attempted to show me how to fish with the artificial fly. Right!

This wasn't so much fishing with the fly, it was more a case of trying to get the lure into the water without catching the damned thing in the grass behind you or getting it stuck in your hat. I wasn't going to remove the hat because I didn't like the thought of a size two hook stuck in my ear.

It was a frustrating experience. Yet, after a while I actually started to enjoy it. I even managed to get the fly more than three yards from the bank, once or twice. The complete lack of salmon made the fishing seem a little pointless but having had time to reflect I now think that I can see the attraction of fishing for a fish that isn't there. You're stood in the river, holding a great length of carbon fibre, looking at some of the best scenery this country has to offer. After a while you get a rhythm going with the casting. A steady pull and the line heaves out of the water. It goes quiet. The line loops past you before straightening and the rod builds up the power, on the return journey you give the rod a thump and it hurls it forward again. It is a lovely sensation, one that I didn't feel much on that first day but one that could easily become addictive. Perhaps that's what keeps those older tweed-clad gentlemen going.

Of course there is more to it than that. Once the cast has been made the actual fishing begins and it was at this stage that I had to admit to my total ignorance. It was hard enough getting the fly into the water and I didn't want to show myself up in front of the others after a relatively successful cast by shouting to Ron - 'Right, what the hell am I meant to do now?'

As a result I spent the morning casting at a salmon river as opposed to fishing for a salmon - I enjoyed myself but I didn't expect to catch a fish. I don't think Ron expected to see a salmon on the bank either.

Fly-fishing for salmon makes your arms, shoulders and back ache. I know that if it's done properly it isn't meant to, but you have got to remember that we were, 'Just coarse fishermen.'

Later in the morning we also span for the salmon and spinning with a lure is something I do know a little about. When I handed over the fifteen foot fly rod and picked up a ten-footer with a multiplier reel attached, I thought that I was, at the very least, in with a chance of actually hooking something and that tends to keep the interest up.

Ron showed us how to rig up a fascinatingly intriguing piece of fishing tackle logic - the floating Wye minnow. He showed us how to attach the banana shaped lead to keep the bait down and add weight to the cast, where to tie in the highest quality ball bearing swivel, and he demonstrated how well the wooden yellow belly lure showed up as it whirled its magic in the murky water. Basically he did the whole thing for us - including some rather dubious looking knots. Still, we had been told that this chap knew what he was doing and I wasn't going to be the one to chew through the line and make a new knot on the grounds that he may have got a little upset.

Weather and river conditions are vital for success in salmon angling although even if they are perfect there are thousands of other factors that can leave the fishing rod straight for periods measured in years rather than mornings. Our first day alternated from bright warm weather (not the best conditions) to dull cold weather (not the best either). In between it was wet and very windy. These were conditions that I wasn't certain were good or bad. We stuck it out, only once joining our hired gillie who appeared quite comfortable drawing on his pipe in the smoke filled Landrover. When Ron asked, 'Do you boys ever stop for a beer?' Some of us had anticipated the question and had already unclipped the waders.

It was good to have a beer with Ron. He knew one hell of a lot about the river, a lot about salmon, about the history of the area and almost everything about everyone who walked in or out of the bar. He also had this annoyingly encouraging phrase that went along the lines of, 'You know lads, there's a real chance of a fish this afternoon.' We liked

Ron and he seemed to like us. After all these years of guiding rich anglers from around the world Ron warmed to us because as he put it, 'We were common.' Prising Ron away from the warmth of the hotel was as hard as the morning's fishing but we couldn't afford to sit there all day.

Back by the river the rain had been replaced by a scythe of wind that sliced deep into tired faces. Ron gave us instructions as to exactly (and I do mean exactly) where to fish. Then, through the cracked opened window of the Landrover he would yell, 'Don't you worry boys, if you hook a fish I'll be out quick enough.' All through the long afternoon we never had a touch.

It was inevitable that we would join Ron in the Landrover to get ourselves warm enough to get out again. One of the lads mentioned to Ron that if (and, believe me, this was a big if) he caught a salmon he would release the fish alive to continue its fascinating journey up the river. Ron drew heavy on his pipe, directing the resulting smoke in our general direction with the sound of a surfacing whale, raised an eyebrow and asked, 'Which bit are you going to let go, the front or the back end? I'm taking my half home!' That sort of ended any conversations about conservation and we got back to the task of trying to catch Ron his supper.

We fished in the same way, covering pools, runs and everywhere Ron pointed in that methodical way I had seen salmon anglers in the past. The river was rising fast and ran as red as a fox. After two days of intense fishing we were without a fish. 'That,' said Ron, 'was the way it went.' After one of those polite pauses that signals the end of a fishing trip, he added, 'Never have had a salmon when it's been that windy.'

Thanks Ron!

With two days without a fish under our belts you would have thought that we would have stuck to fishing for fish that actually eat something when they're in a river. But fishing for fish that don't, seems to have this perverse attraction. I started reading as much as I could about fishing for these damned irritating things called Atlantic Salmon. I thought that this would give me a greater insight into the sport - it didn't. There are so many conflicting views, arguments and theories that I think salmon fishing prepares you for the fact that death can't be the most painful part of life. From all the reading. I extracted the following facts:-

Salmon are not always in the river.

Salmon do not feed when they are in the river.

Salmon only move about in certain conditions.

There are not as many salmon as there used to be.

If you do hook a salmon it very often comes off.

Nobody knows why a salmon takes a bait in the first place.

If this doesn't put you off you need to understand that when it comes to actually trying there are even more obstacles in the way. For instance, there are several ways you are allowed to fish. You can use the salmon fly, a lure, or a bait of worms or prawns (remember, in all these cases salmon don't feed in fresh water - we think!). This sounds reasonable until it is pointed out to you that you can only use these methods at certain times of the year and, on some rivers, you can't use them at all. The time of year you can fish each method may, or may not, coincide with conditions when they are likely to take that bait. Apart from that you can do pretty much as you like - as long as you can afford the privilege of getting on the river in the first place. Basically, salmon fishing doesn't make sense. At the same time it is compelling. That was why Phil and myself were back in the hotel getting ready to go for another try and why we weren't too happy being labelled 'Just coarse fishermen'.

So, we left the posh guy with his cigar smoke for company and went to do some fishing. Settling down on the river at the top of a very seductive pool I pulled the new fifteen pound breaking strain line from the multiplier reel and threaded it through the rod guides. The chances of hooking a fish seemed so remote that the last thing you want to happen is for the thing to get off due to a poor knot, or break you because you were using old line. So I took my time.

We fished wooden floating minnow lures, yellow bellies two inches in length, just how Ron had shown us.

After a few hours I found myself working down a particularly interesting run of water. The lure swung across the steady push of water held at about a foot above the river bed by the banana shaped weight. I could feel the lure revolving freely by a fluttering sensation and I knew it was fishing at the right depth because I could feel the lead bumping across the gravel as it headed towards a big rock at the end of the run. Everything was working so well I kept putting her out.

Phil had wandered off to try his luck elsewhere. I was stapled to exactly where I was, feeling the water at the back of my legs and looking at the river still to be covered, at the hills in the distance and the billowing clouds that framed the image.

The next run through was no different from the dozens before except that something invisible engulfed the little wooden lure and gave it a hefty tug. The unexpected had happened.

It was definitely a fish. The rod swung back and I pinned the bugger. The educational vision of Ron the gillie shouted, 'Hit it as though you want to pull its bloody head off boy!' Perhaps I should of hit it again but I hesitated. The line tightened, it sang and droplets of water catapulted off as if a child had twanged a taught washing line after a summer shower. Out of the water came a Polaris of a salmon. It was not happy.

I've seen this sort of thing on TV documentaries but to be actually standing in a river up to your waist in water and connected to one of these things is entirely different. An amazing sensation and there was no doubt about it, I was into a salmon. Then I was out of it.

Contact to loss lasted just long enough for that fish to project itself from the depths and spit out my lure as if it were a loose strand of tobacco from a badly rolled cigarette.

I have lost fish before, I have felt the shock and disappointment deep in my marrow on more occasions than I care to remember, but this was different. I had just lost the impossible. Losing something that you never thought you would find in the first place is hard. It definitely isn't one of those things you just shrug your shoulders at. Oh dear, it happened all right, it's just that I can't believe that I let it happen. In the short space of time it took for that salmon to flick me to one side a multitude of thoughts kaleidoscoped through my head. Some were vivid, others confusing and some were down right murderous.

It started with a jubilant, 'Jesus, here we go.' And ended with a more explicit piece of blasphemy. In-between I had visions of sauntering back to the hotel, kicking the door open and slapping a 15lb. salmon on the nicely polished bar whilst announcing, 'Not bad for a coarse fisherman'.

Before the dreadful moment I had been debating in my own mind whether or not to kill the first salmon I caught (you can tell by this that I was either supremely confident or one of the world's great dreamers). I couldn't make up my mind. Traditionally all salmon were taken for the table. But times change, attitudes calm and we are left with the feeling that maybe its not right to kill a salmon that makes a mistake.

It is all very well saying this after the event but at the time (when I should have been concentrating on securing a good hook hold on that fish) I have a sneaking suspicion that I was looking around for a big enough rock to smack the bugger over the head with. I really wanted that fish. Maybe it got off because whatever is in charge of fate knew that there was a good chance that I would have killed it. The loss had nothing to do with fate. I have had a great deal of time to try and work out what went wrong - it was bad fishing.

The loss of a fish doesn't stop when the line goes limp. I fished on as you do, but knew it was useless. I had thrown away my only chance (possibly in a life time) and eventually we broke down the tackle and headed towards the inevitable inquisition at the hotel. I felt like the young boy who had to tell his parents he'd been sent home from school.

Fortunately there weren't too many people in the bar and not one of them looked like they knew anything about fishing. We perched ourselves on vacant bar stools, ordered a drink and waited for the hotel owner to show his face.

One of the young local girls was working the bar. The owner was in the kitchen covering for an absent chef. Apparently he wasn't in a good mood. As she pulled the drinks she asked, 'Are you going to cheer Mike up by telling him you've had a salmon?'

I said, 'No.' With conviction.

'You better tell her,' said Phil.

There I was, forced to relate the sorry truth. One or two of the other customers started sounding like fishermen after all as the occasional, 'Oh dear,' could be heard rattling around the oak panelling. Mike appeared from the kitchen, hot, busy and with plates full of local game pie and rounds of sandwiches.

News had obviously seeped through to the kitchen. On his way back he stopped, glanced at me and said, 'Stupid boy.'

I heard him quite clearly.

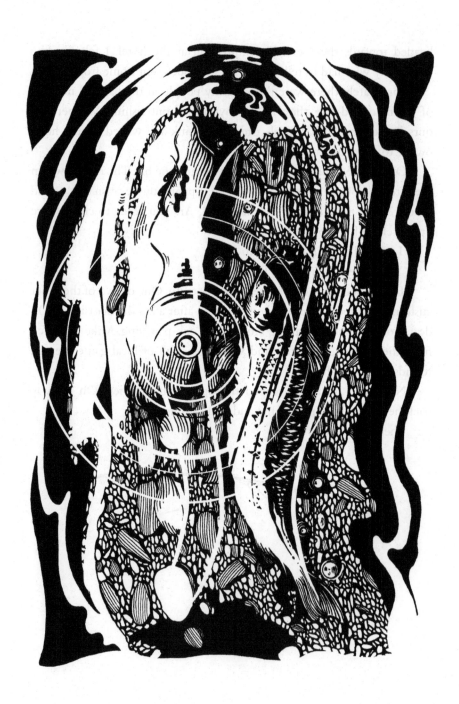

GETTING THE BALANCE

SUMMER FISHING - HEREFORDSHIE

*The reason I like rivers so much is that you are never
entirely sure of what is in them.*

The fascination of the water has got me again. So here I am. It's the
weekend and I'm by the edge of the river. I'm keen to get on with the
fishing but I don't want to hurry. It is so pleasant down by the water that
I think, 'Why isn't everybody doing this?'

The rod is assembled slowly as I look at the current and try to figure
out how much weight is needed to get the bait down to where I've
convinced myself the fish are. I want the bait down there but I don't want
it to be anchored in one spot. It is early summer but the fish have been
unseasonably inactive and I need to search them out, roll the bait right
in front of them and tempt them to take it on the move. It's a nice way
to fish and that is why I'm now sat on a rock trying to get the balance
of the tackle just right when twenty minutes earlier all I wanted to do
was chuck a bait in the river and pray that a wandering fish would potter
upstream and bump into it. I have learned the hard way that they very
rarely do that.

Once the decision on the size of lead has been made the rest becomes
automatic. I have now tied so many pieces of braid to pieces of fishing
line and so many hooks to pieces of braid that I no longer think about it
until it's done and then only to double check that everything's tight and
secure, it usually is. That isn't a boast, it's just reassuring.

It's getting lighter and the landscape is mystically quiet. Everybody else in the country is either asleep or polishing golf clubs in anticipation of their own little obsession. Everything feels right and there is absolutely nowhere that I would prefer to be. I start saying deep meaningful things to myself like, 'Yes.'

A can of corn is wedged into the left hand pocket of my old faded artists' smock, the hook box and a few lobworms are dropped into the right hand one, and I slip down a very steep bank. There is still enough morning dew to make the near vertical descent quick but just before the river I manage to stop, then I gently lower myself down into the cool embrace of running water.

It's deeper than I estimated and, as I wade my way across to a small gravel bar, the push of the water makes me think that sometimes, when I'm fishing alone, I do some pretty stupid things. The sight of the fishing position outweighs the possible danger and suddenly I'm back on dry land on a glorious little hump right in the middle of the river. The view upstream and down is magnificent. I'm embraced by the glow of the early morning and I remind myself that this is what it's all about.

The water at my feet swings in around the gravel bar that has created the little island. It then pushes underneath the trees where the depth increases and the current slows, creating one of those promising areas where the surface just seems to flatten out and where you can trace the crease in the current by the line of bubbles that point the way. The trees keep the sun off the water and make the fish feel comfortable. To get a cast in tight to the bank is tricky and its easier if you wade out into the water a little and perch on a small ledge just before the drop off. If you're wearing chest waders it's possible to actually sit down in the water and get the perfect angle to fish the run from. It looks a bit stupid to the watching herons but it does allow you to achieve what you want to achieve, it gives you the best possible angle from which to present a bait to the fish and it keeps you low to the river where the fish can't see you.

I push a fistful of corn down into the water until my knuckles feel the gravel. My rolled up sleeve absorbs a fraction of the river. The current plucks the corn from the palm of my hand and carries it down, rolling it away into the darkness beneath the foliage. It looks really pretty.

It was time to make that first cast. I released a few more grains of corn and followed their course through the run with two pieces on the hook. That cast wasn't close enough to the trees and didn't trundle through the swim in the right sort of way. I retrieved it, very slowly and without breaking the surface of the water. I removed a split shot from the line and tried again. This was better and the line transmitted the little bumps plucks and flutters that tell you the balance is right. After it had trundled along the bait settled towards the tail of the run. I guessed this was where the natural food collected so I left it for a minute before nudging it on it's way again. As soon as it moved there was a little tug, nothing specific but something that the river hadn't done on its own. The rod twitched back. The hook was set. A fish was on. The fight began.

It's somewhere between excitement and worry. You try to get the fish out as quickly as you can and the fish tries to stay in there for as long as possible. At any time in between something catastrophic could happen – the hook could pull out – the fish could beat you in the tree roots – the line could grind across a rock and part in one of those sickening cracks. It all gets a bit tense. I don't want to get into a debate about cruelty and fishing here (I reckon I can defend it well enough) but a hooked fish would prefer not to be hooked. That's why they fight. And, that is exactly what this one was doing.

The line cut through the surface like wire through cheese and the fish showed her colours as she twisted four feet down and flashed an iridescent broadside like a mirror catching the sunlight. As she tired I looked around for the net. It was fifteen feet away, a typical display of forethought, so, once the tussle was over, I scooped down, gripping her lightly behind the gills and held her in the water as I flicked out the hook point.

This little barbel was a lovely display of what a healthy fish should look like. I held her in the cool current to regain strength before releasing her like a captured butterfly. She flipped away leaving me with a quick shower of water and a smile. She disappeared following the exact route the free offerings of bait had taken. It was a nice sight and I took the time to listen to the silence that had fallen on the river.

There was a pause but the possibility of another fish had me re-baiting the hook, regaining my posture, slowing down my heart rate and trying to avoid the overhanging branches again.

It worked. I caught several more and they all behaved in the same manner and each time I held one, the fascination was the same. These were fresh fish, new fish, they were small, but they were lovely.

I sat back on the gravel and realised what I was into here. A glorious day, the purity of the river and a contentment that I wanted to last for an eternity. It all seemed too good and I half expected a hoard of approaching anglers to come invading what I now regarded as my space. On this morning it wasn't just this little three yard run of water I felt was mine – it was the entire river, and this is one big river.

I knew that I could have caught more of those fish yet I came to the conclusion that there was no point. To flay the place would have unsettled the fish and left me feeling guilty, so I sauntered across the deep, fast, dangerous water that had bothered me earlier and raised myself back onto dry land. I felt like God.

Instead of fishing elsewhere I kept gazing at the river I had just left. It held a tight grip over me and, as I looked, I realised that my perception of what I wanted from a river had just snapped into clarity. I recognised that what spiralled past me ten feet below cascaded into a piece of water that held everything that a young fish could desire. I was looking at a run of water that was the very future of the river and with this knowledge I could begin to bring the river into some kind of perspective. Now I could see through the layers of uncertainty and I realised that all those monster fish I had been chasing over the years weren't that important. What really matters, what really makes me go fishing, is the river herself.

RON'S STONE

FISHING GUIDES - THE RIVER WYE

*If you happen to be in the way when a seasoned
fishing guide starts talking it is best to listen.*

The river Wye has its source high up in the Welsh mountains and ends in the Severn Estuary well over 150 river miles away. That's a lot of water. It's good water too. 'Grade One' is how the scientists label it. I tend to look at it from a fishing point of view and regard it as the most interesting single body of water I've come across on these Isles. Give me the choice of only one river to fish and I would snap up the Wye before anybody else could answer.

It's the variety that does it for me. Up the top end you can fish for the grayling in the winter and the trout in the summer. The middle reaches simply scream barbel, chub, perch and pike and as she winds her way down to the sea the roach and bream shoals start showing their potential. There are other fish too, fascinating fish, like shad (the May fish as the old boys call them), bleak, dace and then there is the salmon which I have a particular affection for because it's the only one I haven't caught - yet!

I adore this river, all of it apart from a 50 yard stretch through the centre of Hereford where the local youth spit on canoeists as they glide under the bridge. I can even put up with that as long as I remember to keep my hat on and realise that this is just a blip on an otherwise fine illustration of what Nature is capable of. It is a big, beautiful river, but with so much water where do you start if you want to catch a fish?

Well, we all find our favourite stretches and most of us like to keep them quiet because that's exactly how we like them. And yet, even on the popular stretches, you can find those little patches that you can begin to regard as your own - you know, the ones you don't fish when others are around. I've worked in advertising most of my life and if it has taught me one thing it's how not to advertise. But I also like to think of myself as not too selfish, so, I will tell you about one little place that was shown to me by a man who has worked the river for a considerable amount of time. His name is Ron. I'll even give you a little clue as to where this place is. Unroll a map of the entire Wye catchment area. Ready? This place is about four tenths of the way down from the source on a right hand bend. You can't miss it. It's so obvious, or at least it was to Ron. Personally I had walked past it on so many occasions that I am ashamed to admit it. I had to get Ron to show me the exact rock that he had talked about in the hotel lounge several years earlier when he'd taken me on a failed trip chasing one of those Wye salmon. He reckoned it was the best rock in the river because that's where the salmon rested when the river hits the one foot two inch mark on the gauge by the bridge.

There weren't any salmon in the river when Ron showed me the stone but he puffed on his pipe, blew the smoke high into the still evening air scattering midges in the process and muttered, 'The barbel like it too.' He then gave me that look that said, 'You 'ain't that interested in the salmon - I know exactly what you are after'. He was right too. I had just been handed fifty years of experience in five words. Ron then walked upstream leaving a trail of spent matches as he tried to re-ignite his pipe. I stared at that rock for a long time before catching him up. He was sat on the trunk of a fallen tree looking intensely across the river where the surface of the water humped over an unseen obstacle and where a kingfisher was looking from her vantage point with keen interest.

'They get in there too, but that rock is the place when the river is at this level,' he said.

Ron's stone is pretty small for the reputation he heaped on it. As the river swings around it shallows up. In the summer there are those luscious flags of weed waving their shadows over the gravel. The current leans to the far bank and picks up speed as it cuts under the wooded bank before levelling out over more ranunculus and slowing into a pool where the cattle like to cool down in the summer heat and refuel. They stir up the mud and dislodge a lot of insect life from under the pebbles whilst drinking. That can be a good place too.

Ron's stone is just under a foot wide, one and a half long and fourteen inches high, sort of mid-way between a rock and a stone and, yes. I have measured it. It's not so much the stone itself that is so interesting in fishing terms but what it does to the current. This stone doesn't intend to be moved so the water is forced to heave around it in low water conditions and rolls right over when the river is up. Behind, decades of erosion have dug a nice depression which attracts fish like a light bulb attracts moths. It looks absolutely fantastic down there.

When the river is low you can sit on the rock (sorry Ron) and trundle a lobworm through the weed further downstream. When it's up you wouldn't even know it was there. Personally, I like it when you can't really see it from the bank but you can see the gentle boil on the surface it creates when the gravel is being stirred up and you can rest your right boot on it and get a nice comfortable fishing position when all those caddis are being washed out of the gravel and the fish are sheltered from the current. Basically, this is one the best swimfeeders the river Wye has ever seen.

So, does this stone really attract those fish? Of course it does. Ron's no mug. As a professional guide he knew exactly where the salmon would lie because if he caught his client a fish it was more than likely that he was going to get himself a tip. He just happened to pass this particular tip on to me and it was a good one. As Ron so kindly pointed out, a feature like this one in a river appeals to more than visiting salmon.

Since that walk with Ron I have studied that stone a great deal. The more I look the better it gets. Minnows hang in the slack directly behind it in a tightly packed cloud that moves as one and the shadows of patrolling chub occasionally glide across the visible gravel. There's plenty of natural food down there which makes it very attractive from a fishing point of view. I have managed to catch a few small barbel from behind the stone and a few sightly bigger a little further down, where the current speeds up and the river bed shallows. This little patch of the river is like the classic salmon pool on a miniature scale. I find it very hard to pass by when the river levels are suitable and there is nobody else about to see what I am trying to do. For all my enthusiasm though I have yet to contact one of the bigger fish.

They do get in there, I've seen them. Big barbel that hug the bottom effortlessly in the rolling current, wheeling around occasionally as they intercept some item of food that the turbulence has dislodged. The problem is I haven't worked out a way to get out there and stay quiet enough for a fish to feel comfortable enough to take the bait. It's a real challenge, a test of your approach. You need to get as close as possible to control the bait but keep far enough away not to spook the fish. The shallow wade across is gravel all the way, and to sneak up you have to be very careful because there's no bank-side cover either. It can be hard wading when you're crouched down that low. It's exciting but its hard. It would be all too easy to give up on the place but I still fish there in the hope that I might get the approach right. Mostly I fish there because it's a nice place. It's a good rock. It's just that either the fish aren't always there, or they were there and I scare them off. Trying to get the balance right is so tricky. Although I haven't figured it out yet I do have an idea whirling around my little head that just might work.

A few years ago I was privileged to fish in India with a river guide (Ron's equivalent) called Subhan. This man's mastery of his river is legendary. Some of his approaches are mind blowingly simple - always dangerous. I adored his approach.

Now one of the things Subhan showed me was how to use a rock to position a bait without the current affecting it. It was so obvious I hadn't even thought of it. What he did was position the bait by hanging the line across the rock itself. I watched him do it time after time at unbelievable distances and with spectacular accuracy. It was an inspiration in fishing ingenuity. I am not saying that the Wye is like the river Cauvery in India, or that the barbel behave the same as the mighty mahseer that rule that river but they ain't that far distant - just a little scaled down in both cases. Now I reckon that I might be able to get one of those larger, more wary fish, from behind Ron's stone.

Naturally I will have to try this when nobody else is about, partly because of that advertising thing but mainly because I don't want to get laughed at for purposely snagging up my line on a rock. Of course, I'd look pretty good if I actually hooked a fish but then everybody else would start doing the same thing and that wouldn't be too good for either the place or the fish. Maybe I am a bit frightened of trying the idea at all. What I really need to do is get Subhan over from Karnataka and Ron from wherever he is now and watch two of the best river guides I've ever met solve the problem of a little rock in a big river. And, if you still think I am selfish for not drawing you a detailed map of exactly where Ron's rock is, let's just say that this is the river Wye - there are thousands of rocks out there. Find your own.

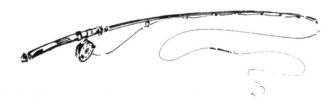

Ron no longer guides on the river and, sadly, Subhan is no longer with us.

THE POOL

Having neglected the fishing rod during adolescence
and 4 years at art college I moved to London where
a chance meeting had me digging up worms.

Every true angler conjures up a secret place. A place in which to spend his endless days. A place where the fish never stop growing, where the only sounds are the plop of his float and, after a very short pause, the screech of his reel confirming contact with yet another monster. This is a place where the fish leap and swirl to greet him in the early morning and where they sulk in the dense weed as he turns for one last glance on his journey home.

This is an image which has been passed down through angling literature from generation to generation. It's all very romantic stuff and it is how all of us fishermen like to view our pastime, yet fishing consists of bad times too. Of days when the rain is cold and horizontal, the sun far too bright, or the stream you have decided to fish is polluted, dried up or packed with other individuals who thought about the potential of the place around about the same time as you did. Even so, against all the odds, it is possible to stumble across a place that retains the essence of all those early books, a place that makes all those hard days worthwhile and downright necessary. I have been fortunate, I've stumbled into a few of these places over the years, but the one that got me in tune with what fishing in its purest sense is all about was the place that my great friend Rod Green simply ended up calling 'The Pool'.

I had been introduced to Rodney by his parents whom I met after

I had moved from the quiet of a Yorkshire village to the madness of London over thirty years ago. They discovered that I had been to art college, was working as a commercial artist and, seeing as how I wore long hair and tattered Levis, decided that I would get on with their son for the simple reasoning that he was working in the same industry, and had even longer hair and a pair of jeans that his mother had been threatening to put in the bin for longer than she cared to remember. This was no guarantee that we were going to get on. As it happened we did.

Along with our similarities in careers we discovered that we had both fished as children and both neglected the rods for more adolescent adventures. After a great deal of talking the inevitable happened. Old tackle was retrieved, we bought some new line, a few packets of hooks, a bright red tipped float apiece and a couple of rod licenses from a musty old tackle shop in South Woodford to keep things nice and legal. We then dug up a few worms and went fishing at the Wake Arms Pond in Epping Forest. We fished through the night, got cold, and didn't catch a thing. It was a little taster of what was to come.

Ambitions were reduced and the next weekend saw us at Highams Park where we fished for the tench in the shallow water between discarded supermarket trolleys and stolen bicycles. We fished just as we had as kids - big floats, big hooks, big lumps of bread for bait and a bucket full of expectation. The only difference was that we stopped for a beer on the way home instead of a bottle of Tizer.

This time we caught some fish - small, plump, beautifully smooth, glorious tench. It all came flashing back and now, as each weekend crawled around, we shook off the restrictions of adulthood, became children and went fishing.

Being beside water was infectious but everywhere we fished there seemed to be rubbish strewn on the banks and too many other people around for our liking. Fate intervened as we became friendly with a chap called Philip Hurley who (purely by coincidence you understand)

belonged to an exclusive local fishing club. This organisation had access
to waters that not only looked the part but offered some fantastic fishing.
This club was so revered it had a waiting list for membership. I can't
remember exactly how, but we bypassed that waiting list. I do remember
that it took a while, a bit of lying, a lot of pleading and what seemed
a great deal of money, but we managed to become members of the
hallowed club and shortly afterwards we started to catch fish, real fish,
big fish by our standards.

As a result I got a little obsessed with the truly fantastic tench fishing
in the Lea Valley at that time whilst Rodney always wanted to catch
himself a monster pike, just like the thirty pounder that hung in a bow
fronted case above Phillip's living room fireplace. Then we stumbled
upon the pool.

When I first set eyes on the pool the skies remained dull, no rainbow
appeared and no fish leapt in and out of the tranquil surface as they
should have. Yet there was something about the place that slowed you
down. Something that allowed you to lie back in the tall grass and do
very little but drift away and look at a brightly tipped float. It wasn't
spectacular fishing but it was fishing in its purest sense - a case of going
fishing rather than catching fish and, every now and again, tiny pin-prick
bubbles appeared on the surface, reeds nudged as the fish moved through,
the float nodded and then sailed away under the slipstream that divides
air and water and we hooked a fish. I could have lived there.

I have always thought that small pools have an embracing quality
that the large expanses of water just aren't capable of and this pool was
a perfect illustration. As a result we fell in love and began to haunt the
place. We did alright too. We caught rudd, roach, perch, bream, tench
and a very strange looking chub. All the same, it wasn't the fishing that
was so special, it was the place. It was one of the few places we found
where no one else went. No one else gave it a second glance because it

looked so insignificant to those who had left their imagination behind in childhood. In reality this pool wasn't really a pool at all. It was an area of the larger gravel pit that was cut off from the rest by trees and a thick reed bed. The overgrown banks encircled the pool but a little channel connected it to the rest of the gravel pit. You could crawl into this oasis and lose yourself. It was quite beautiful.

Generally it was the tench that we were after and then Rodney struck into a fish that stretched his line right across the pool and smashed him leaving a thread of disgust to flutter back with that sickening realisation that you have just lost something pretty big in a small place. We guessed it was a carp. As a result we went tench fishing hoping for a carp and carp fishing hoping that there was still a chance of picking up a bonus tench. It was a compromise. It was great fishing. Nice and casual.

As the long summer days drifted into autumn the pool changed character and the water took on a dark intensity, that hid the beauty beneath, as the calm waters were highlighted by a carpet of rust coloured leaves that defied perspective, like one of those crazy Escher drawings. The undergrowth thinned, the reeds crackled in the breeze, the weedbeds withdrew and the pike arrived. We were waiting. At this time of the year the small rudd and roach migrated to the pool from the adjoining bigger water and the larger pike followed, pushing their way through the reeds like grazing elephants, bullying their way into our territory. You could hear them.

Rodney cast his live-bait to the edge of a decaying weedbed. It wobbled the cork float. As it worked it's magic he waited for something miraculous to happen. It took a while but when the float thumped down my friend struck, made contact, and found himself attached to something weighing considerably more than the usual eight pounder we had become accustomed to catching. I missed the action. I had gone for a walk with the float rod to try and catch us some more bait. Typical!

When I got back the fish lay on the grass. It was the biggest thing I had seen outside of the covers of Bernard Venables magical 'Mr Crabtree Goes Fishing' book that I had read almost every night as a child. We were escalated into another league. This was almost a twenty pounder and, twenty pounds (we had been told) was the mark of a specimen. The pool had shown her potential and we looked at that fish in awe. This was a proper pike, thick set, powerful with eyes the size of a dog's and a set of teeth to match. After a great deal of admiration we released the obvious monarch to her domain. It took the two of us to lower her back into the water and when we did she lay in the margins for a while and then, puffing some air out of her gills, she sauntered off brushing through the weed like a farmer walking through a wheat field. We looked at each other and smiled.

Not really expecting to make contact with another fish Rodney mounted *my* last live bait and cast it very casually, very precisely, to where the big fish had made her strike. I remember thinking that any other pike would have fled during the commotion but I was wrong. The ripples the cast had created had only just disappeared when the float did the same and there Rodney was, bent into another fish - bastard!

This time I was with him to give advice, to help steer her away from the dangers of the snags we'd got to know so well, to give encouragement and to get ready with the inadequately sized landing net. This is probably why he lost her.

She'd been on for what seemed an eternity. At first she stayed deep and unmovable, then she showed her speed and powered for the sunken tree to our left and we cringed as the rod moaned as it tried to turn her. There were big boils underneath the surface that lifted the water and rocked the reed beds. This was an obvious monster, larger by far than the one we had just returned, but we never saw her once. There was a crack like a pistol shot, the rod bounced back and the line twanged in our general direction. Everything went quiet and then Rodney summed up our feelings poetically with a bit of blasphemy that would probably be censored if I repeated it on the printed page. He then threw the fishing rod down in disgust and the pool returned to her normal tranquillity as if nothing had happened. It was impossible to estimate the size of that fish but, using the first pike as a gauge, well, let's just say it was big.

We fished for that fish for the rest of the season. The eight pound pike we caught didn't seem good enough any more. Looking back, that was a dreadful shame but all we wanted to do was get the fish that we had lost. It all became obsessive, we wanted her that badly that whatever the weather, whenever the opportunity arose, we hounded her like Captain Ahab chasing Moby Dick. We tried everything in the book and a few things that weren't but she had learned her lesson, she was a clever one. Whatever we chucked at her she simply ignored. I dreamt of that fish so much that I don't remember waking up until the end of the fishing season. My dreams and daytime thoughts spiralled around the pool. I could smell her, visualise her and I craved to be in her embrace every hour of every day. There was a power to that place that grabbed me so tightly that, when the end of that fishing season arrived, it was a relief. Fishing was never meant to be that intense.

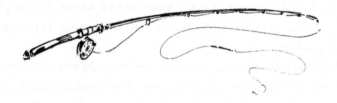

TWENTY POUNDS OF FAITH

PIKE - THE LEA VALLEY

I have heard it said that fishing is a religion.
If that's the case then I met my God many years
ago on the banks of a little pool in the Lea Valley.

I was meant to have been designing a prestigious annual report for a company whilst pretending to be 'arty' for the sake of the client. Instead I was looking out of the window at the weather which, of course, was absolutely perfect in fishing terms. The corner of one eye was staring at a photograph of a pike caught the previous season around about the same time of year and the other was looking at the clock. This was no way to carve myself out a career, but I really didn't want to be there. That clock moved incredibly slowly, more of a delayed jerk than precision rotation and always at its most unpredictable on a Friday. It happened to be Friday.

Something that *was* predictable sauntered into the studio, glared at the clock, made suspiciously polite conversation (as bosses do at quarter past five on Fridays) and asked, 'Any chance you could work the weekend?'

'Absolutely none,' I said.

I offered no excuse. Telling him I had to go fishing would have been like his blind date calling him the following day and purring, 'Ever so sorry, I just had to wash my hair.'

There was a fair amount of fumbling with bits of paper whilst he waited for me to weaken but before he could re-phrase the question the clock had reached the half past mark and I had gone.

Once out of the building I dumped the car at home and met my good friend Rodney for a beer in a particularly grim North London boozer. He wasn't looking himself. There was a worry dragging through his mind that took a good two pints of cold 'light and bitter' to get out by which stage he told me his father had been taken into hospital.

It was one of those moments when you wished you hadn't asked. I should be able to talk about these things to a friend as close as Rodney but I found it awkward. I talked about fishing instead and, as I did, I watched him mellow like someone easing themselves into a hot bath. The end result was that we agreed to try the next morning for one of the pike in a pool we knew. It was one of those conversations that has you clapping your hands and saying, 'Right, let's get on with it.'

The following morning we dredged our way through grey suburbs, parked the car, chucked the rods out and things brightened up. Expectation had kicked in. We were going fishing.

When we got to the pool she was enchanting. Her perfume was seductive in the moist morning air. Autumn leaves carpeted her banks, there was no breeze and the water had an ancient musty smell clinging to the surrounding trees along with the cobwebs. It was going to be a good morning. Sometimes you can just tell. Knots were tied and tested for a strength to conquer monsters and we started fishing with feeling. We tried by the reed beds, in the margins, in all those places we had seen pike before, and in all those others where you just mumble, 'There must be one under that tree.' We covered a lot of water in a small space. The intimacy of this pool was perfect.

Rodney ended up in the undergrowth on top of a steep bank where his ability to get caught up in the trees could be observed from the opposite side of the pool. I was making a similar fool of myself at the other end. I am no brilliant pike fisherman but I have to say, Rodney can be. He has a certain empathy with his quarry that makes him search out every little place a pike of any size is likely to be holed up whilst waiting for some dumb fish to become breakfast. This was mobile fishing. Exploratory fishing. Dangerous fishing. Exciting fishing. It is inevitable with this approach that even if you don't get a fish you get pretty tired and a little cut up. I like that too. It can also prove expensive when it comes to the replacement tackle department.

I adore fishing overgrown waters for pike. If you don't have to force your way through undergrowth and untangle fishing rods from branches it just doesn't seem like hunting. It's all to do with the predator instinct. Because of the pre-historic nature and looks of the pike (and the adrenaline created when trying to track one down) piking is more like hunting than fishing. It is something that gets you moving very slowly, avoiding cracking twigs, creeping up on menacing looking depths and sharpening hooks in a way I am sure our ancestors used to. I can't see Neanderthal Man roach fishing from a punt, but I can sure see him after a pike.

By mid-morning I was cursing at a newly acquired laceration on my forearm. Rodney was suspiciously quiet, so I wandered back to check how things were going whilst licking my wound (as you do when you haven't caught anything after an hour or so).

There he was, crouched down, rod in hand, an eager look forcing itself past the brim of his hat, cigarette discarded on the ground, tensed up, ready for what I knew he was going to do, then - whoosh - he did it. The rod swept back. He leaned into something living, glared at me, grinned, returned the cigarette to his lips and got on with the business of trying to control whatever was on the other end of the line. He can be so bloody casual at times but that fish brought him down to size forcing him to give line and one of those worried glances that say 'Uhm... you wouldn't mind popping over here and giving me a hand would you?'

The correct procedure to one of these silent pleas is to saunter over, peer into the water and casually pick up the net. This gives the impression that you've seen bigger fish than the one that is flapping about down there. I couldn't. This fish was really going for it and, no, I hadn't seen bigger fish.

My partner was hauling into her but she just promenaded past in a display of 'Have a look at what your dealing with boys before you start thinking about any bullying tactics.' It was a vision that had me fumbling with the net and wondering when Rodney was going to let me know when he wanted me to net her.

'Not yet.' He answered, even though I hadn't said anything and then off she went on a circuit of her domain like an athlete doing a lap of honour.

Rodney's superb choice of fishing location had allowed him to find, present a bait to and hook the fish. It had not taken into account how I was meant to get down and net her. This is an illustration of when the one holding the rod realises who his real friends are and the one holding the net wishes he was holding the rod.

The battle was similar to all those that you can read about in any 1950's fishing book except that this one was personal. When it got near to the finale I had to make a decision. Well here we go. Slip onto the crest of that ridge, keep a tight grip on the net and gently, slowly, lower myself six feet down onto that sturdy little ledge.

The operation took half a second. It was also further down than I had estimated. That sturdy little shelf collapsed before I hit it. The water was cold. The net, which had decided it liked being tangled up in the brambles, was persuaded to release its grip and joined me with a slap.

The fish was still on. Rodney was still smiling. The water was now very cold. Now here comes the dangerous bit. Your friend is up there with the glory. You're down here with the responsibility. Net the fish and you're a hero. Lose it and well...

Netting that fish was like scooping out a dream from the depths of my childhood. Rodney heaved up the prize and took her to the safety of wet grass. I was left slopping about in the water. The fish had been landed. Rodney was still smiling. The water was now at frostbite level. I was left down there in the mud for what seemed like a week at work before a hand grabbed hold of my arm, hauled me out and I was able to look at the fish.

She was a beauty. Rodney was quite emotional. I wanted to say, 'For Christ's sake, it's only a fish,' but it came out as, 'Well, there's our twenty pounder.' As I shook the hand of my friend there were tears in his eyes. I was congratulated on my netting technique and I pointed to the fish as if to say, 'Well, you caught her.'

We sat on the grass, then, rather clinically, we reduced an obvious masterpiece to pounds and ounces and took a lot of photographs on the grounds that you only catch your first twenty pounder once. As we lowered her back into the water she melted away like an uninterrupted dream. Sinking into the depths she kicked her tail into first gear and glided away. Rodney told me that he caught that one for his father.

That fish had a great effect on me. Getting the image of her out of my mind was hard. I got absorbed in pike, pike fishing and the history of the sport. I had the fever. Even now, all these years later, when the air smells sweet, I get this urge to ring my friend and say, 'I was thinking about going to the pool just once more.' 'So was I.' confirms a feeling that telepathy may be triggered by a combination of enjoyment, senses and memories that may just be able to bend spoons.

Big fish are great, we all love them, yet the essence of fishing is an emotional thing. That pike from the pool was a landmark for us in terms of shear bulk but it was the initial belief that led to the meeting. It wasn't determination, perseverance or being in the right place at the right time or even luck that caught that fish. It was our faith in her existence.

Years later, after I had left London, I wandered into the local bar in Cheltenham. The usual hard core regulars were on their allocated perches. The crossword had been completed. The conversation wandered into one of religion.

'Best keep out of this one,' I thought.

They rambled on about Jesus, Buddha, Islam, persecution, charity and all the usual alcohol induced philosophies. There were no raised voices, slamming of fists or those things that make you nervous in confined spaces, so it wasn't too difficult to sit and listen and slow down after yet another week at work.

Inevitably my opinion was asked. I explained that I was not a great believer, not a great fan of the church as an institution, yet I could understand the faith aspect. In unison, like a polite, middle class, church going congregation, they questioned, 'How?'

I was forced to equate something that I didn't know much about, to fishing, which is a subject I know a little bit about. So I told them how I used to fish with a good friend in an overgrown pool that was dismissed by most as only containing small fish. I explained that this place had a calmness that could be described as spiritual, somewhere to be regarded with intense respect, like their church. As time passed the belief in the invisible occupants became very strong. A religion if you like. Once we caught that fish our faith was rewarded. When we held her we were, to all intents and purposes, holding our God.

My explanation had the small audience mumbling something along the lines of, 'Isn't it about time you got your hair cut boy.' Then it went quiet, so I tossed in, 'Well, at least we let our God go!' That stunned them for long enough for me to leave without being crucified.

Shortly after that morning of magic when Rodney caught the fish his father died.

A Rather Large Fish

SALMON - THE RIVER WYE

Sometimes it can seem a pointless exercise. Then,
as a fish crashes into your life, you are reminded of
why you are doing it in the first place.

I had been after a salmon from the Wye for so long I had almost lost the will to cast. I had grown used to looking at the river whilst hoping for the unlikely and filling in the disappointment by calculating how many miles I had walked in pursuit of an illusionary fish. Of how many expensive lures I had lost to rocks, how many flies to trees and how I always drove home without a fish. But this day was very different. I had got myself a salmon.

Now, I know that in these enlightened days of conservation we are encouraged to return any salmon we get but I'm sorry, this one was coming back with me. The fishery owner knew that too because he helped me carry the beast to the car and lent me a thick blanket to cover it up so that nobody in authority could see what we were doing. This fish was so big I had to put the back seats of the car down to get her in. After a quick handshake and a glance around for any bailiff who might be popping into the hotel for a beer, I crossed the bridge with my salmon. I drove slowly, as if I had a delicate piece of Chinese porcelain as company but not so slowly as to arise suspicion, like a driver who knows his tax disc is out of date.

Arriving at home I unwrapped the fish and Helen and Tom admired her in the full glory of daylight. The jaws of a young boy dropped as he looked at something almost as long as him and with a girth that made him look positively stick like. The fish weighed a staggering 42lbs, was 47 inches from the tip of her nose to the fork of the tail and a tape measure wrapped around her on capture had shown 25 inches. To say my family were impressed is an understatement but I still didn't gain hero status. You see, I didn't actually catch her.

Even though she looked as fresh as if she had just come out of the river she was 89 years old. She was killed by a Mr Geoffrey Cornewell on the 20th of April in 1920 and was hooked on a two and a half inch Reflet minnow. The word 'killed' instead of 'caught' suggests it was the gillie who hooked her and Mr Cornewell who wallowed in the glory. What I was looking at was a beautifully painted life size portrait of a magnificent fish that had come from the river Wye and had been beautifully executed in watercolour and gouache by a certain Cecilia Goulburn after it had been executed by Mr Cornewell. I had looked at that painting every time I had visited the fishing hotel and had always wanted to pluck up the courage to ask how much they wanted for it. I need not have bothered. It wasn't for sale. I know that now because the owners of the local estate had asked the landlord the same question the previous week and the answer was a very definite, 'No'. They did, however, ask if it were possible to have the fish copied and that's why I ended up with her.

At first I thought I could take a series of photographs in the hotel and then stitch them back together through the clinical mathematics of Photoshop, having her reproduced by a very good digital printer (with some very expensive machinery capable of holding all the detail). It didn't work because of the reflections of the tripod on the glass and we couldn't take her out of the oak frame because it was too risky and we might have damaged her. After a week of research I found a solution and that is why, after a great deal of uncertainty, I had been allowed to take her away.

After a lot of technical talk a friend called Richard Gray and I photographed her in eight sections on a copy stand so we could get the camera dead level. We lit her with lights which had polarising filters attached to get rid of those awkward reflections. We then put her back together, piece by piece. We handed the resulting image to the best retoucher I know who took out a few specs of dust, some scratches on the glass and a couple of wrinkles in the paper. There was still a lot of work to be done, like matching up colours, along with paper choices and other details that can drive you mad and cost you quite a bit of money too. Before it was all done I had to return the original to its rightful owner so I drove up to the Wye and, just to keep things nice and legal, I put my salmon back, like a good boy.

A week later I was back to do some proper fishing. I had a week's holiday with my friend Phil Humm which involved a car load of fishing tackle and a Canadian canoe. We had rented a cottage close to the river and the plan had been to have a couple of days with the fly rods and then go barbel fishing at the beginning of a new season. I had an offer to go salmon fishing on the river Usk on the first day but, as I pointed out to Phil, firstly, I was on holiday with him and secondly, if I were ever to catch a salmon, I wanted it to be from the Wye. I knew the statistics and conditions on the Usk were more favourable but that is how I felt.

On that first day the sun was very bright, it was hot, humid and the river was carrying quite a lot of colour although it appeared to be dropping out, well, that is what optimistic minds told us anyhow. As we got the tackle out of the car I realised that I had brought the wrong fly rod so I got back in the car and returned to base to pick up the one I wanted whilst Phil walked across a field to begin fishing. I returned about half an hour later with the rod I should have taken in the first place and a salmon spinning rod just in case we saw one. Phil had. 'A small fish,' he said. 'Just underneath that bush on the far bank.' She had stuck her nose out and, just like a good gillie, he had seen it. I left her for about 20 minutes as I tried fly-fishing for a perch that was chasing some fry and, after I failed in that department, I put up the spinning rod, pulled the line off the multiplier, added a Wye lead, an extra swivel, a three foot leader and attached a two and a half inch yellow belly floating wooden minnow. I then walked upstream as quietly as gravel allows to get an angle on the place. I had a few test casts to get my range, then I moved down to where Phil had marked her.

Third cast, as I could feel the lead plucking over the gravel run, and the minnow vibrating in the current as it spun its spell, I had a steady pull so I pulled in the opposite direction. I had pinned my fish. Small or not this was my salmon and I hauled into her because I didn't want to make it my 'possible' first salmon on the grounds that I have already done that twice.

I was cool, calm, collected and a liar so I shouted, 'Phil!' He looked up, realised I wasn't kidding, and sprinted ashore as quickly as waders allow throwing his expensive fly-rod down and picking up the landing net in one swift movement, like an osprey grabbing her own catch. It was going some but I continued to bully the little fish until that little fish boiled on the surface and turned into a big one. It was one of those 'Uh. Oh!' moments. Phil looked at me as if to say, 'Careful boy.' And I looked at him to say,' I'm trying to be.' He then said he was going to get his camera to take a shot of me playing a salmon and I said, 'I'd rather you stayed here with the net.' I think he got my drift.

The fish had its own idea of what to do and tried to get as far away as possible from the two idiots standing in her river. The fight goes on and on in my mind but we got her in eventually. Phil lifted the net, the line went slack, the rod resumed the straight position, the hook fell out and we had our salmon. I say 'ours' because that was exactly what she was. Phil spotted her. I hooked her. We both landed her. It was a very firm handshake to seal the first fish of a week's holiday.

She looked fantastic - fit, broad and muscular with a flick of purple across her face and a sheen that ran along her silver flank, just like in that portrait. The sun shone brighter, kingfishers streaked down the river as if in an air show and the buzzards hung amongst the angels to get a better view.

From then on it got a little technical as we looked at the wooden minnow (that had some impressive teeth marks cutting through the paint work and a rather more worrying bent hook). I am now sure that if that fish had leapt out of the water we would have lost her but we hadn't. I knelt down at the alter of water she had come from and kept smiling. Phil started dancing about and singing 'Rob has got his salmon' and I kept thinking, 'Yes, I have.' It was a lovely moment.

After photographing her we held her in the water whilst she recovered. A couple of canoes drifted down and one of the day trippers asked us what we had caught. I said, 'Salmon' – with authority, giving the impression that this was an everyday occurrence for such a superhero. Phil lifted the fish out of the water for them to see and they all said 'Jesus Christ!' That was a good moment too.

Once recovered she reacquainted herself with her fascinating journey and we realised to the full what we had done. What a creature and an obliging one too. She hit the minnow around about 11.20, we released her about 11.40. I know that because I looked at my watch as we watched her go. Phil knows that because he saw me looking at the watch which prompted him to say, 'I suppose we had better go for a beer then'. I had already started to break the rod down.

As we floated across the field I kept thinking how simple it had been. We saw a salmon, gave her a little time to relax, made the cast and latched into the unbelievable. So easy that it had only taken me seven years.

As we drove to the hotel I mentioned that the glass of beer ahead of us was going to taste as good as that one looked in 'Ice cold in Alex'. Phil suggested that I may be having more than one. I did too, and why not. Hell, we were on holiday.

Once we had settled in at the bar Phil asked the landlord if anybody had had any salmon off the stretch this year (before showing him the display screen on his Nikon). He had now. He looked at me over his spectacles, extended a hand and said 'You'll have to catch one on a fly now.' He bought us a beer too.

Having caught more salmon off the Wye than I ever will he asked us what we thought it weighed. We guessed between 15 and 18 pounds. He scrutinized the screen and said 'Maybe a little more, hen fish too.' We then had some more beer and I started to bore people with the story, over and over again. I'm still doing it, that's why I am telling you. I have caught plenty of fish in my life but this one was special and what really sealed it all was that Phil was with me at the time. It was right that he was there. He has always said that I would get one eventually and eventually needs celebrating. We did not do much more fishing on that first day and, in the evening, Phil entered into the cottage guest book – 'Day one, Rob had an 18lb salmon – not a bad start.' At the end of the week he wrote 'Went downhill from there on in...' It doesn't matter, that fishing trip will be remembered for the moment when two fishermen and a fish came together. A time when excitement thumps through the body as the dramatic scenery of the Wye valley falls silent as if admiring what she is capable of.

On returning home the image of that fish stayed with me and it wasn't long before the majority of people I met, or talked to on the phone, or happened to be in the queue in the butcher's shop knew about that fish. I could not contain my happiness. When people asked me why I was smiling, I told them too. Others looked on and said 'I've already heard' but they obviously didn't fish or were just plain jealous. The moment is still with me and will be as long as I have a pulse. Even though we let her go I can see every detail and, as I looked at the test print of that huge Wye fish from the 1920's I shook my head in awe just as I had with my own salmon. My fish may have been far smaller but the colours were as vibrant and the feeling of excitement when I saw her safely in the net must have been the same as that Mr Cornewell and his gillie had all those years ago.

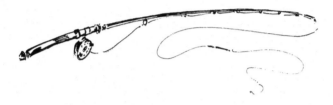

That 'salmon' of mine caused quite a stir. Some thought (and still do) that it was not a salmon at all but a sea-trout. I remain unsure. If it were a sea-trout it would have been, to my knowledge, the largest sea-trout ever caught from the river Wye - some nights I find it hard to sleep.

DON'T SPOOK THE FISH

WATCHING FISH - HEREFORDSHIRE

*There is only one thing better than catching fish
and that is watching them before you try.*

A few years ago, I was taken to a stretch of the river Wye by a good friend of mine. He is the only person I know who has permission to fish the stretch, but hasn't had the time to take full advantage of the privilege which, at first, seems an awful waste. As a result, the stretch has hardly been touched in fishing terms and can only be described by any level headed, mild mannered, perfectly normal polite fisherman in one way - it's sodding beautiful.

If it were possible (which it is not) for man to design the most perfect piece of flowing water, this would be the model for it. This place is simply magnificent and 'No!' I am not going to tell you where it is. Sorry!

I know that I will never get to fish this bit of water. I also understand the reasons why and there is absolutely no way that I will poach a piece of water when it has been shown to me out of respect. I console myself with the thought that there still exists some stretches of undisturbed water, on this most beautiful of rivers, where the fish are left in peace. Watching fish behave naturally in such circumstances is a wonderful thing to do, a real privilege and yet every time I think about the place I start looking for loose soil where I might find a worm but I have to remind myself I can't. I do promise I will never fish this stretch (unless the owner changes his mind) but I will not give in to the rebel inside me that says that it would be really nice to spend an afternoon looking at the unobtainable. Furthermore, if I do happen to get hauled up in front of the local magistrate, I may well use this paragraph to bolster my flimsy defence.

This stretch has everything you could hope for. There are the classic pools that have the salmon men drooling, deep still holes underneath overhanging trees that surely hold gigantic pike and places where it would be lovely just to be allowed the privilege to stand in the water and feel the current dig the gravel from under your feet.

Whilst we were meandering about that afternoon, we came across a cluster of barbel feeding close to the bank. Here, the power of the river is channelled through a gap so narrow it seems impossible for such a large river but they were holding there just fine. The light was not perfect (in fish spotting terms), but once we had focused into the multi-dimensional world of water, it was fairly easy to pick out one or two large fish in amongst the others. One in particular was feeding away quite happily in the faster water, probably on caddis. It was like watching a chicken picking up loose grain.

When you see fish like this there is an automatic pondering of just how would you set about catching one of the damn things. If only you could get the permission to try in the first place. It was whilst doing exactly this, that all the fish got twitchy and started behaving differently. At first, I thought we had given ourselves away but then I spotted a couple of canoes making their way down the shallows several hundred yards upstream. There was no doubt about it, two brightly painted canoes were about to pass five foot over the heads of several happily feeding fish. This was going to be disastrous.

The barbel had sensed the canoes well before I had yet they didn't seem to mind as much as I imagined. As soon as the canoes glided towards them the fish simply melted away. There was no panic. They just stopped feeding and moved to one side, in the same way a child would stop eating an ice cream if the Red Arrows decided to do a low fly past on a quiet Sunday afternoon. We waited to see if they would reappear. They did too. It took them about the same amount of time as it would have taken for that child to realise that there was something dripping over his thumb and the ice cream needed finishing.

Now, a lot of people may say, 'So what!' Well, in its simplest form, the observation at least allows you not to get too upset when you spot a fleet of canoes beaming down on your favourite barbel run so it will cut your cursing down a bit. But I got to thinking that I might be able to turn this little observation to my advantage. After all, those barbel were feeding quite happily before the disturbance and continued very shortly afterwards. It occurred to me that if I had dropped a bait down to them at either of these stages, the chances are that it would have spooked the fish simply by casting in. Fish are very good at picking up noise and vibrations and, when you consider that sound travels five times further under water than through air, the sound of a bait being cast in must be like someone slamming a door.

I started to reason that the best time to put a bait in was as the canoes went over their heads. Not before, not after. The returning fish would surely come across the bait without detecting the noise of the cast because the disturbance of the canoes had moved them out. When they returned they would come across a bait that appeared totally natural and was not accompanied by the heavy splash that usually delivers it. It is very unlikely that a bait behaving naturally would not be accepted by a feeding fish - whatever the bait! It was one of those 'Eureka' moments that is so obvious you need to prove it is correct.

The following weekend I was back on the Wye, not that same stretch I am afraid, but on the river all the same. I was fishing my usual way, travelling fairly light and trying to cover a lot of water in a short space of time. I do tend to weigh myself down with the camera equipment but I'm not going to leave that behind because I enjoy the photography, too.

It's a simple way of fishing that can be very productive. I am not saying that this is an approach that works on every water, just that it's an approach that has worked on every water that I have fished. Others do it differently and pin their hopes in a single place. They catch fish too, but I can't help thinking they are missing out on something. When you have access to six miles of river and only fish four square yards of it, it seems to me that you are limiting your options, if not wasting good money.

Whilst I was walking the river, I came across a spot where a branch had snagged on the river bed several years earlier. It isn't a huge feature, but every year a little more debris get attached in the winter floods so it has become part of the river's topography. The fish have grown to like the security it offers. The downside is that there is a high steep bank behind it, so approaching the place usually scares the hell out of the fish because, as you attempt to creep up on them from upstream, the bank crumbles and big lumps of earth tumble down to announce your arrival. If you try slipping over the top, they see you. The fish usually lie very close to the bank, so you have to be very quiet or sit there for several hours until they arrive. I don't have several hours to wait for something that may not happen and I was about to dismiss the place when I remembered those canoes.

I flicked in about twenty grains of corn, one or two at a time, which settled behind the snag and then left the place alone to fish elsewhere. After a couple of hours, I returned and crept up on the place like my life depended on it and edged my head over the rim of the bank. There they were, five barbel that I could see. They were feeding on the corn, picking up a grain and wheeling around in the relatively slow current taking up position a few yards downstream, whilst the next fish had a little nose about. At times like this I get very excited and automatically reach for the rod but I knew that would be catastrophic.

I knew that if I made a cast the fish would disappear. I have seen it happen more times than I care to recall. Remembering the observation from the previous weekend, I looked upstream for a canoe to come around the bend. There weren't any but I was determined to wait for one - the noisier the better. Actually, one of those stag parties that come down every now and again would do fine.

The weather was great, no rain, warm, still, sunny enough for shirt sleeves. It was the weekend too. Not brilliant conditions for fishing but perfect for slashing down the river in a canoe or two. I looked at my watch. It was 11.30, just the time most canoes arrive here after they have set off from Hay on Wye. In between looking upstream and saying, 'Come on.' I kept sneaking back to see how those fish were doing and flicking a few extra grains of corn in to keep them interested. They were very interested. There was still no sign of a canoe.

I thought about fishing upstream for a while until a canoe swung around the bend but I got a little paranoid that someone else would turn up and see the feeding fish, so I stayed where I was, underneath the tree, stoking up the Kelly Kettle and making a mug of tea. With nothing but time on my hands, I changed the tackle, substituted the lead for a stone and placed the hook length so a single grain of corn rested on the stone. Still no canoes.

This was ridiculous. It was now 12 o'clock, all canoes come through at this time because they are trying to reach the bridge at Bredwardine so they can get out, walk up the hill, and have lunch at the Red Lion Hotel.

12.30. Still no canoes.

Right, that was it, despite all my plans, I was going to have a cast. I couldn't hold back any longer and decided that the hoped for stag party had got stuck further upstream at the Boat Inn above Winforton, where they were probably having a bite to eat in between drinking contests.

I got up from under the tree with the rod and a half empty can of corn. As I did, I spooked a couple of swans which took flight and made their landing just where the barbel had been. They adjusted their feathers, hissed in my general direction and then floated off downstream. My first thought was, 'That's all I need,' then I thought, 'That will do nicely.' Sneaking up on the place, I had a little look over the ridge. The fish had gone but that was no surprise. I slithered over the high bank, crept up as close as I dared, lowered the bait into the water and then hid the best I could by keeping low and waited for the fish to return. It didn't take them long and they immediately started grubbing about again. It is hard to hold your breath for too long but that is what I tried to do. These fish were so close I could see the excitement in their eyes. One of the smaller fish smelt the bait on the end of my line, grabbed it as though it had been on hunger strike and the fight was on. That single grain of corn was resting on the stone I was using as a weight and she simply sucked it in and wheeled around.

There was a scramble along the bank then the fight took me into the water as she headed for the snag but I managed to turn her. It was a great feeling of achievement and patience on my part and that is quite unusual. But it had worked and a lesson had been learnt.

I am now convinced that the best bait for catching a fish is caution. If you can creep up without spooking them, if you can merge into the landscape, if you can walk across gravel quietly and avoid casting shadows over the water, there is a very good chance that you will catch one of the creatures you have been watching for so long. A lot of people ruin their chances of catching a fish simply by the way they approach the water and, when they nail a couple of rod rests into the gravel, it makes me cringe and curl up as if someone has just run their fingernails down one of those old fashioned school blackboards.

There is a lot of uncertainty in fishing. The one thing I am sure about is this. No matter how careful you think you have been, the fish know you're there.

If you can get a bait to the fish without spooking them you're in with a chance. If not, you are going to have to sit there for a very long time and that, quite simply, is a waste of good fishing time.

BEFORE ROCK & ROLL

CHILDHOOD - YORKSHIRE

*I have always believed that to enjoy your fishing to
the full it is essential that you fished as a child.*

In the beginning God gave us fish. A little later on he got around to creating children. To ensure that the two came together he produced catapults, minnow traps, worms, marmalade sandwiches, wasps, pocket knives, Intrepid Black Prince fishing reels, granny knots, wet feet, thermos flasks, barbed wire, poaching, bailiffs, fields and freedom.

Somewhere down the line he created parents so that us kids could have access to all these delights and then He tossed in the miracle of a phrase, 'I'm off fishing.' This gave the parents their share of the freedom and God could have a rest too. It was all very well organised.

Scientists and religious leaders have complicated this simple process of evolution with theories and schism throughout the course of history, but this little list of pictures is all I really remember about the beginning.

My memory is like the stroboscope at a Youth Club dance, it allows me to glimpse fragments when I really want to remember the whole thing. Most anglers I have met can recall the first fish they caught - I can't.

The uncertainty has obsessed me for years and I'm left believing it was either a whiting from Bridlington harbour, a stickleback from Driffield Canal, a very odd looking creature from a rock pool in Cyprus or my brother's pet gold fish (called Guppy) that lived in an enamel kitchen sink that my father had sunk into the turf and that all us youngsters knew as 'the garden pond'.

I hope it was the goldfish. At least then I could rest conscience free, knowing it was returned alive because I remember with crystal clarity, releasing it in the sparkling stream near our house before the Royal Air Force had the family on the move again. A similar fate was not awarded to either the whiting or the stickleback, and a bronzed Cypriot boy ran off with the other specimen around about lunchtime.

I put my loss of memory down to the fact that I stopped fishing around about the same time that I noticed girls through the flattering hypnotism of those disco lights. To attract the girls you had to adopt a more grown up attitude to life than fishing allowed. There was no metamorphism. No probationary period was allowed. One Saturday afternoon you were fishing, the next you were sprucing yourself up for the local Youth Club dance. It was exciting and, although I wasn't very good at it, I did learn that the words, 'I thought I'd try and catch a bullhead from the beck,' is not the best reply to the request of 'What are you doing on Sunday?' Especially when it came from the only girl in the room who possessed breasts.

I found it a great deal easier to get my hands on a bullhead than that girl. There were too many eager competitors buzzing around whenever she bounced around in a manoeuvre that could have been the origin of the phrase 'With a spring in her heel.' There was no doubt that the effect was dramatic, but so were the colours of those little fish. I can picture every detail of that bullhead right now. I can only recall two things about the girl and one of them isn't her name.

Fishing rods gave way to hair styles, Rock & Roll, lust and red tag Levi jeans in the adolescent dream of making yourself a lot older than you actually are. Fishing was for children. Your hormones told you that.

Looking back, those childhood days of fishing were magical. The essence was simplicity. The purpose of the exercise was to have fun and it still should be. Catching something was merely a bonus so it was impossible to fail. To become a 'successful' angler it's relatively safe to say you need to catch your fair share of fish, but to enjoy your fishing to the full I believe that it is essential that you fished as a child.

Before I started looking at girls I fished whenever I could. I even got drawn into buying the all important fishing accessories that you don't really need. At the time these were things I craved. Tasks like the local butcher's round turn you into a capitalist before you're ready and I remember spending my hard earned cash on a set of Junior Samson Pocket scales and one of those fishing knives that were housed inside a crude wooden ruler with true inches marked on one side and the more generous fishermen's version on the other. They were fun too, but I wasted my money. None of them helped me catch a fish and I rarely used them for the purpose described on the packaging.

I wasn't doing anything special. It wasn't a big deal for a boy to go fishing. It was natural. We all did it. Good days were measured in how far you could cast. It was as simple (or as difficult) as that. From my observations, men of beer-drinking age did this with apparent ease. They crouched behind reeds and beat every cast we'd ever attempted with beautifully engineered centrepin reels, a casual flick of the wrist and a puff of the pipe. Floats behaved as they were meant to and fish were hooked. Generally this was the only fish we saw out of the water so we moved our tackle closer to where the miracle had occurred and asked if we could borrow a maggot – 'PLEASE!' The reply was generally short.

Those beer drinkers could certainly cast a line but they sure found it hard to smile when a swarm of eager admirers moved in for the kill. Being the youngest of the fisher-boys I couldn't run as quick as my elder brother or his friends. It was my brother who really went fishing. I just tagged along – the young whipper snapper to be watched over as my parents killed two birds with one stone as they got both of us out of the house at the same time. I hope that whatever my parents did with their freedom was as enjoyable as what I did with mine.

Fishing wasn't as straight forward as just turning up. Sure, we had all acquired a rod, a reel and a length of line with more knots in it than was healthy, but there was more. To tempt a fish you need a bait (actually, you need to find the fish first, but you learn that later). Bread was our favorite. My brother's friend was the son of the local baker and we didn't have to pay for the stuff. With bread, there was no real need to watch the float, you just glared at the white dot in the shallow water and hoped beyond hope that it would disappear as some fantastic creature engulfed the offering. We did use other baits like slugs, caddis, elderberry, cheese and, very occasionally, when the pocket money allowed, maggots. For a few seasons everything clicked into place and fishing became part of my everyday life. Then God looked down on this little piece of creation and decided I was enjoying myself too much.

Through divine intervention my brother spotted a girl through a stroboscope and that was that. I was dismissed for the encumbrance I'd been for so long. I no longer had anybody to fish with because all his friends seemed to have spotted girls at the same time, so with nobody to show me what to do I had to work it out for myself. I watched those fish and, ever so slowly, I began to catch a few. I started to approach the water carefully and to think before I made a cast. It was hard fishing alone but something deep inside kept me going and I began to catch all sorts of fish and each and every one became fascinating.

The perch felt strangely dry for something that spends it's life in water; an unexpected revelation like finding out that a snake isn't slimy or that you came into existence as a result of your parents having sex!

A pike was frightening. Even though I adored the way they dragged the huge battered cork float across the surface before battle commenced they always made me feel a little nervous. Unhooking them wasn't a problem because, I am sorry to say, I followed the local custom at the time and killed every one I caught with a rock and cut them open to get my hooks back. I'm glad I didn't catch too many pike. And then there were the roach. Oh the roach was the top prize, the holy grail. They were the challenge, they were glorious, and yet, despite their beauty, I remember thinking they were weird. They have this peculiar smell which is more vegetable than fish. Now, I don't make a habit of smelling live fish but once you've smelt a roach you can't forget it, and in a similar way that the first freshly cut lawn tells you it's summer, your damp hands tell you it was definitely a roach that you just let go. Forget the scale count, the differences in the lower lip and the angle of the lateral line that the biologists talk about, a true roach smells of roach and not of a roach/ bream or roach/rudd hybrid. Even a ten year old knows that.

There were more fish too, fish from an all together different place. A place where grown-ups wore tweed trousers (that were neither short nor long) and flayed the swift shallow river with expensive wooden fly-rods for hour after fishless hour. Despite the amount of money they paid to get on to that river they obviously didn't know how to fish. I never had too much trouble extracting a trout or two on a worm. The bailiff never seemed to fully approve of my tactics although he must have sympathized because he never once tried to stop me. I suspect he just couldn't be bothered. I also think that he quite liked seeing young kids down there. Often, he could be seen (from a safe running distance) resting on the trunk of a fallen tree where he would stroke his dogs and look in my direction for worryingly long periods of time. He hid a smile behind plumes of tobacco smoke cascading from his pipe into the still air of evening.

My Woolworth's fishing rod took me to some marvellous places. Places that adults ignored. Summers were long and warm and there was always something to do. Then it happened. The luminosity of clear streams and lily clad pools was overpowered by cheap disco lights and the fishing tackle was left in the shed. It stayed there until I'd been through the period that involved motorbikes, Jimi Hendrix, experiments with herbs, a thump on the forehead that really hurt and a regrettable incident that involved a 177 Diana air rifle, me, and the local solicitor's son before I moved away to art college.

The pubescent period of school was over and there I was at art college with a short academic record and a lot longer hair style. My specialist subject should have been, 'The history of angling art.' Or, 'The English Dawn and how it reflects in water.' As it happens it was just about anything that came into my head which wasn't a great deal.

All that time when I was searching for something really important to paint or photograph, fishing never flipped back into my mind.

Years later, far away from the countryside I loved, working in London, I picked up a fishing rod again. It felt comfortable, as though it had been tailored, and that glow of youth seeped through the cork handle, up my arm and back into my heart. It felt real good.

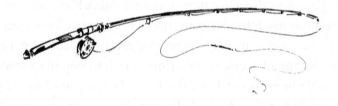

THE CLUB

A MOST EXCLUSIVE FISHING CLUB

*My fishing turned full circle as my childhood tutor
became the club chairman.*

I hated fishing clubs so much that I formed one. I admit that at the time I didn't really know what I was doing. Still, nobody has got themselves killed, nobody has been thrown out for not wearing a tie and nobody has resigned. The formula for this success is simple – there aren't any rules. It isn't exactly anarchy, but it does allow me to say that maybe, just maybe, I don't hate all fishing clubs. Just most.

All the ones I've been a member of are full of the committee type people who do more talking about fishing than actual fishing. I understand that some things need discussing and that some of the things discussed need sorting out, but when the reason you have joined is for the social side of things rather than access to a particularly tempting bit of water, then it is time to take up golf. Golf societies have loads of committee meetings.

So, why did I even think about the idea? Well, there was a little lake nearby that was up for grabs at an affordable annual fee to any 'interested fishing club' – no individuals need apply! I wanted to fish the place so I formed a club. I didn't get the water but I became so accustomed to the idea that I began to hold my head up and say, 'Sure, I'm a member of a fishing club – is that a problem?'

This was all a long time ago, a time when I had become disillusioned with the whole fishing scene. Things had changed and the attitudes and the competitive element that accompanied the 'big fish' scene didn't suit my childish visions of what this supremely simple act of fishing was all about. Everybody I met just wanted to play the waiting game until some monster carp (and usually it was a carp they were after), finally made the mistake of the year and found itself tethered to a sleeping individual that gave it about as much respect as he gives the waiter in the Indian restaurant at 11.30 on a Friday night. It just didn't seem right. Like a lot of things, we'd messed it up.

Fishing had become something it was never intended to be - it became hard and I became fished out. The angling scene had me answering those social statements like, 'I can't see the point of going fishing,' with, 'I'm not sure I can either.' It wasn't good.

I eventually snapped out of it and managed to tempt my old friend Rodney over to Ireland for ten days fishing. In the meantime, I had met a bunch of guys in Gloucestershire. They were good company but I fished differently from them and they thought I was a little weird because I only used one rod.

I had agreed to fish one of the gravel pits with these chaps one weekend. Things got planned, tackle and bait arranged and then I got a phone call from Rodney who said that it was about time I came down and fished back in Hertfordshire. I had to go. I wanted to go. But I also had to wriggle out of the arranged trip. I was puzzling over an excuse in the Brewers Arms in Cirencester one lunchtime when one of the Gloucestershire boys bounced in announcing that he was really looking forward to the weekend. It is at times like these that you wish you could crawl away and hide under a stone to do whatever things that crawl away with any frequency do.

'Look.' I said. 'I've got a bit of a problem here and I may not be able to make it.'

'Why?'

'Well, I have got to go back to London for the weekend.'

'Why?'

'Well, I belong to this fishing club... I've been invited to fish in a match... I just can't refuse.'

'Why not?'

We were getting on reasonably well considering one of us was disappointed and the other one a dirty-lying-son-of-a-bitch. Then he figured me out.

'But you hate match fishing.'

'Yeah, I know, but this is a really exclusive club... not the usual sort of thing... it's kind of traditional... expected... you know.'

'What's this club called then?'

'Crimson Quill Club - fancy another beer?'

There was one of those voids in conversation that have you fiddling with boot laces and brushing the remains of a bag of crisps off your jeans whilst I kept thinking 'nice name that,' then I got another question hurled at me.

'Exactly how exclusive is this club?'

'Oh, very.' I said.

So the club was formed. This was to be a very exclusive club; myself, my friend Rodney and Phil Hurley (with whom I used to fish with in those days). A membership list of any more was more than the administration could cope with. Apart from that, very little changed. The club was simply three friends fishing together. It didn't mean anything unless other people wanted to make something of it. Human curiosity being what it is other people did start making something out of it. In Gloucestershire I got quizzed more and more. I couldn't let on because there was nothing to let on to, so I just started a good clean bit of exaggeration - as fisherman are meant to.

Suddenly the Club had mythical waters, a fact substantiated by the 'CRIMSON QUILL CLUB Private Fishing' notices I started to carry about in the back of the car (the ones that appeared, just out of focus, in the photographs showing the lucky member wallowing in delight at his latest capture).

Rodney was doing the same and was winding up one particular chap in London who had connections with The London Fly-fishers Club. I have forgotten the name of this character but he was one of those golf-club-committee-types in the respect that, if such a society, club, association or organisation was in existence, then he had to be part of it. His jacket was covered in little enamel badges and the rear window of his Volvo with membership stickers. The lure of an exclusive angling club was simply too much for him.

News filtered back that he had caught a magnificent carp from the King George Reservoir. Had this, he wondered, qualified him for membership? Absolutely not. This seemed to rub him up the wrong way because he said something along the lines of, 'Well, you can't be a real club because you don't have a chairman.' A bit of a childish attitude I thought, but I suppose he had a point so we decided to get ourselves one.

There was only one possible candidate. So I wrote to a well known artist, writer and fisherman who was the hero of all fisher-boys born in the 1950's, and asked Bernard Venables if he would be our Honourary Chairman.

Two days later I received a delightful letter and we had ourselves a chairman. The chap in London never really believed that Bernard was our chairman until we showed him the letter of acceptance and the Christmas cards he had sent us. We still didn't let him into the club.

My fishing turned full circle as my childhood tutor became the club chairman. We all went out and celebrated with what can modestly be described as, 'Quite a lot of beer,' – I think.

That was a long time ago but the club still exists if in name only. It even expanded a few years ago when I invited Phil Humm to join. There was no committee meeting about this, I was fishing and communicating with

Phil on such a regular basis that he just evolved into a member and that's how these things should be. I can't see the club getting any bigger, I like the exclusiveness of the thing. We don't actually do anything under the banner of the club, we never have, it is just one of those things that exists and it remains just a nice little thought to be a member of what must surely be one of the most exclusive fishing clubs in the world.

Our chairman sadly died on 22 April 2001 at the age of ninety four and I suppose that was the end of the club in the real sense of the word.

Bernard was a wonderful character. A super hero in his time. A man who had travelled the world and caught monster fish but who was just as happy catching gudgeon from a Wiltshire stream. I corresponded with him enthusiastically. He always replied immediately. The contact was infectious. Eventually I completed a painting honouring his acceptance into the Crimson Quill Club, a kind of elaborate certificate. I was simply trying to return some of the joy that Bernard had given to me.

I finally got to meet Bernard at an angling show held at the National Exhibition Centre in Birmingham. It was a dreadful affair - overcrowded, noisy, full of people wearing baseball caps the wrong way around and a hideous display of corporate logos.

In amongst all the hype, there he was, an elderly gentleman radiating enthusiasm for the pastime he had cared for all his life. He stood, a little frail, like an ageing rose amongst a bed of thistles.

Despite all the rehearsing I wasn't sure what to say. I just ended up walking towards him and said, 'Mr. Venables... I would like to shake your hand.'

He looked at me as though I was going to mug him.

I introduced myself as, 'Robert... from the Crimson Quill Club.' His guard dropped. He smiled. He held onto my hand firmly and introduced me to the other people on the stand as, 'The man who had sent him the lovely painting.' It was a very proud moment for me, it was lovely to be shaking the hand of the creator of all those books that I used to fall asleep to. We talked, then we went for a beer and we talked a little more.

I never did get to fish with Bernard but we did a lot of letter writing and we got on pretty well considering the age gap. I told him the truth about the foundation of the Crimson Quill Club (which was something he found highly amusing). I talked to him about this book and that all I wanted to do was pass some of my own enjoyment on to my son. He simply said, 'You must do it.'

After a while our correspondence slowed. Bernard's eyesight was deteriorating and that was a tragedy for a great observer. Even so, he kept himself busy by writing, trying to paint and fishing. The three great loves of his life. I stopped corresponding on the grounds that I didn't want my enthusiasm to tire him out.

The last time I saw Bernard was on his ninetieth birthday. We talked briefly over a glass of beer and some very delicate ham sandwiches. He asked if I had finished this book. I told him that I wasn't sure that it would ever be finished.

Bernard said, 'Everything has an ending.'

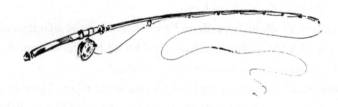